"Well mate, if you want my advice take a lo⟨ opposite then I'm pretty sure you'll do alrig⟨   t

I was giving a bit of perspective to Eden, m⟨ the right choices with his life. To give you a nearly 54, I've been married and divorced twice, I've got 4 kids with 3 mothers. Put it this way, if you landed on my profile* on a dating app you'd be swiping left quicker than you can say car crash.

My son has been pecking my head for a few years now about writing a book about my life. And I've said the same thing. Next year mate. And well next year is here. I uumm'ed and aaah'ed for ages about what I could write about that'd be of any use or interest to folk. And then I had the genius idea of this book - a compendium of my blogs. The book has already been written. And yes it's a little bit of a cop out, but wait there's new material in here too. And even if you end up chucking the book in the bin or on the fire you'll be happy in the knowledge that ALL the profits from the sale of the book will go to Operation-Shanti. Win-win, no?

So 2022 was a bit shit. No, scratch that. It was a lot shit - but it's not *all* bad.

2023 will be a good year. There, I've said it. I never say stuff like that - but it's a promise I've made to myself. The Ashtanga Yoga School project I've set up with me Ashtanga mate Donna Southwell starts in January. It's been 12 months in the making, and if I do say so myself, it'll be ACE. I've finally accepted myself as a good teacher. Maybe I faked it til I made it, but the imposter syndrome is (nearly) gone and I've realised I have certain skill sets as a teacher that can be of use and value to students.

2023 will also see the re-launch of Yoga Manchester (which will be shortened to Yoga Mcr - more snappy for the kidz). When I first started teaching in eighteen fifty three - well it was actually 24 years ago I set up Yoga Manchester - which was the cleverest thing I've ever done - well, truth be told it was actually my web guy who suggested it, as *Yoga* and *Manchester* were the first two words folk were gonna put into google. Yoga Manchester was a collection of classes across the south Manchester burbs. After a few years I added more classes and got teachers in to help me out. We were Manchester's yoga go-to for a while. I added Yoga Express - 45 min express yoga classes for people on the go in the Northern Quarter and also after a spell in London (and Los Angeles) I set up Yoga London Club. Call me His Imperial Majesty, for I had me a Yoga Empire - well not quite. As I mention in the blog 'Shit Happens' this empire ran a little like Fawlty Towers and I was Guru Fawlty. But it was my empire, however Fawlty, and I set it all up through a lot of hard graft and a soupçon of Manc blag.

Cue Darth Vador music: *bom bom bom ba ba bom ba ba bom* - the pandemic arrived and said Fuck You to us all, and all my many years of hard graft got flushed down the covid toilet. Like a lot of teachers I moved the classes online which was ok for a while. Eventually after a couple of years, (the new) normal service resumed. Except my lil yoga business stayed shut. I was stuck in the arse end of England - just kidding Ramsgate, I love you, really. Ramsgate: where yoga teachers are 2 a penny and people much prefer getting off their heads rather than standing on them. What to do? Sometimes you can't see the wood for trees and after a heart wrenching separation and impending divorce I saw the light and the light said 'Re-launch Yoga Manchester you knob.'

So watch this space. Matt Ryan is back in da Manchester house and he is gettin yoga bizy. Yoga Mcr (City Centre Stretching**) will begin again with an amazing city centre studio in Castlefield. Daily classes for everybody, and there'll be meditation classes too.

Manchester, I love you - I am back and I am ready.

* In the last 3 months I've signed up to 3 separate online apps - gone in, added photos and a biog, and then deleted within maybe 40 seconds tops. 3 times... I kid you not. I have 'nuff respect for folk who manage to go on dates via these apps and find love/friendship/ bonking partner/whatever, but it's not for me. I'm too cynical, for better or for worse - cynical and single, but still fabulous.

** I came up with this tag line one day and wasn't sure about it. But actually I think it's pretty cool. The non-cosmic reason is that it takes all the 'bells and whistles and esoterica' out of yoga - you know, the "come find your true self' stuff that puts folk off. I want to make Yoga Mcr as inclusive as possible. This book is meant to show how yoga has helped me change my life for the better and how I truly believe yoga can help most, if not all, folk in some capacity however big or small - you just got to come to class and I'll help you. And no you don't have to wear lycra or even be able to touch your toes.
The cosmic reason it's a good tagline is this: I believe people (*not* the yoga practice) are inherently spiritual. Unfortunately, this all gets covered up over time through familial and societal conditioning and various life experiences. Stretching the body in every which way can help peel back the layers of shit, as can sitting still for periods of time. I make sense of the word spiritual by breaking it down to 'being in spirit' - or the more familiar 'being inspired'. Being in spirit or inspired to me means being a little more at peace with oneself. We are our own worst enemies, or as my Zen teacher Brad Warner says 'I can push my own buttons better than anyone else I know.' So when we stretch our bodies in a yoga session or sit down and be a bit quiet in a meditation class we can catch glimpses of this inspiration, this being in spirit, this being at peace with oneself. How do I know? Well I've spent the last 24 plus years road testing the whole yoga n mediation shebang and I can

categorically say without any BS it's worked. And it can for you - come to class and I'll prove it.

Addendum
Yoga MCR Update May 2023.
After the best part of 3 months of (re) launching Yoga MCR I came to the rather galling conclusion that unless I could find an extra 10K for marketing I would be basically pissing in the wind trying to make things happen. Folk were coming to class and loving it , but just not enough of them. I knew I was doing something right , but just needed more money to spread the word and in the end I didn't have 10K , I didn't have any money unfortunately. And so Yoga MCR would have to close its doors (again).Lesson learned.Get bigger marketing budget next time...

All thoughts comments etc in this book are my own. The blogs were written at various points over the last 20 or so years , so context is everything. I'm sorry if you are offended by anything, but offence is only taken never given.

Front Cover design by @loosecollective
Photo by @anniefengphoto

For more info @mattryanyoga

Prologue...

Matt Ryan gets Operation Shanti Ambassador status

January 2023

When I got the email from Operation Shanti letting me know I was being put forward as an Ambassador for them I was completely bowled over. I've not achieved too much in my crazy life, but this went straight to the top of the list.

I met Tracy, the lady responsible for setting up OpSha, in Mysore around 2003. I'd bumped into her a couple of times at Swami Jamanagiri's Shiva Cave Temple on Chamundi Hill. We'd sit silently and watch Swamiji do his daily puja routine, then all three of us would have some chai and chat.

Tracy likes to keep out of the limelight but she is an incredible person – to have set up Operation Shanti pretty much single-handedly in a male dominated country like India is nothing short of a miracle. She is now Spiritual Godmother to my daughter Agnes Boo.

So fast forward a couple of years to 2006, I was helping OpSha out on a regular basis. I guess my main job was playing with the children, which being a big kid myself was, as you could imagine, simply brilliant. I'd show them a bit of Yoga then they would 'wupp my ass' at cricket – before, I would run rings round them with my silky footballing skills (I, like all males my age, still think I could play professionally).

A few years later the 'big move' happened which involved the kids being taken off the street and into the Karunya Mane home on the other side of the city. Not only did the kids get a new home they also got to go to school for the first time in their lives. Being able to witness this incredible transformation of the children was awe inspiring. There was a little downside to the move for me: my mates were at school and I only got to see them on Sundays – I was Billy Nomates during the week!

In 2011, the OpSha kids were 'guests of honour' at my 'Hindu Style' wedding at the Shiva Cave Temple. What an amazing day to have all my best mates attend my wedding – the video is priceless.

Each time I go back to Karunya Mane, I see their faces light up when I walk through the door. This alone is worth going to Mysore for. To be able to watch them grow up over the years has been both an honour and a privilege.

ALL the profits from the sale of this book and I mean *ALL* will be donated to Operation-Shanti.

For more information on Operation Shanti, its history, mission, and how to donate please go to the website www.operation-shanti.org

Ashtanga Yoga is nothing special (and neither are YOU)

November 2015

Ok so a few blogs back I've written a piece called The Supreme Ashtanga Yoga and now I'm hitting you with Ashtanga is nothing special. I guess you are a little like W.T.F.?

As most folks know I've been 'complementing' my Ashtanga Yoga practice for a good few years now with this Zen thing which basically entails looking at a wall for an hour or so a day, almost the complete opposite of jumping around on a rectangle shaped piece of fabric getting hot n' sweaty. But the more I do of both, the more they morph into the same practice. The quotes from all the Zen masters about zazen (the Zen form of meditation) that I read could also apply to the Ashtanga practice I do.

This is my latest favourite Zen bombshell...

"No matter how many years you sit doing zazen,

you will never become anything special."

— Kodo Sawaki

Kodo Sawaki was my Zen teacher Brad Warner's teacher's teacher. He pulled no punches and told it how it was. Imagine rocking up to an Ashtanga class and the teacher saying something similar..

'Hello there I just wanted to let you know that no matter how many years you practice Ashtanga Yoga, you will never become anything special. That'll be £7.50*, please.'

Would you ever go back?

But what exactly does Kodo mean when he says *you* will never become anything special? And should we believe him? I explained in my last blog exactly why I got into yoga in the first place and it was a case of needs must rather than any urge to become anything special. I guess we all like to think of ourselves as being special in some way and perhaps being told that you are not special is a bit like an elbow in the solar plexus – ooouff. I could get a little cosmic here and turn the whole thing on its head by saying actually you are special, special in that you are completely unique - like everyone in the world is unique.

My interpretation of what Kodo is saying is that the practice – be it yoga or be it zazen – is not something to turn you into anyone special or important. You can try and make this happen, but you won't succeed.

If your practice becomes all about trying to 'find something,' 'seeking mind' as Kodo would call it, you will create an in-balance (which is gonna be extra tricky when you're doing the standing leg lifts boom boom!). If you start a practice wanting that practice to make you happy, like perhaps you think buying that new pair of shoes or new car will 'make you happy,' then you have materialised the practice, turned it into a commodity. Practice for me is about just doing practice. Yes, sometimes doing your practice makes you happy, but what are you going to do when it doesn't? Turn to Hot Yoga? Surely not (jus kiddin hot yoga fans).

There is another Kodo quote about zazen practice. He says zazen is the self 'selfing' the self – er what? *The self selfing the self*? I had to reread that a few times before I started to understand what it meant. When we practice Ashtanga Yoga we are just being who we really are, not seeking or expecting anything – practice for practice sake. Can you do that? You might not have a choice. If you practice for fame and fortune you will soon realise that it aint coming. It's a bit like pushing, pushing, pushing to get your leg behind your head, then when it happens it's a massive anti climax. After a couple of anti-climaxes the penny drops, or maybe it's the ego that gets dropped, and eventually you will get to a place where the practice is doing YOU.

I'll leave you with a quote from one of the world's happiest people. Read it through and see if you can apply it to your Ashtanga Yoga practice, be it a posture that you can't do or perhaps a wrist injury that won't heal.

Remember that sometimes not getting what you want is a wonderful stroke of luck

— Dalai Lama XIV

* this is presuming you live in the North-West of the UK. If you're reading this 'darn sarf' please change this to 25 quid or however much a single yoga class is these days south of the border.

Moon Day Schmoon Day

October 2019

So the Full Moon and New Moon days are auspicious times of the month – especially so, it seems, for practitioners of Ashtanga Yoga. When I first started practicing Ashtanga many moons ago (insert eyes looking up emoji!) I was told in no uncertain terms that I must not no matter what do my practice on Full Moon and New Moon days and that a fate worse than death would be waiting for me if I did. When I delved a little deeper to find out the reasons for this 'rule' (a rule which incidentally out of the many, many different yoga practices only affects the Ashtanga Yoga discipline) I found out that the potential of injuring oneself was much higher on the Moon Days apparently and that one should take rest on these days. *There were also more esoteric explanations check out Tim Miller's Ashtanga Yoga Center website for one.*

Now let me make this clear: I am not in any way suggesting that these Moon Day explanations are not true, what I am saying is that they are not true for me. I've studied the evidence and to be honest the numbers just don't add up. I guess this might in part be due to the fact that being born a Mancunian part of our DNA is not to believe anything or anybody. Well maybe it's a little more like, if it looks like bullshit, walks like bullshit, talks like bullshit, then it's probably bullshit.

My reluctance toward Moon Day Mania started the very first time I went to Mysore nearly 20 years ago. As I remember the Full Moon fell on a Wednesday of my first week, but there was a big sign in the Shala saying that Moon Day (ie the Shala was going to be closed) was going to be on a Thursday. Wow, I thought to myself – the might of Pattabhi Jois – he has the power to change the lunar cycles. I was then told or rather someone whispered to me behind closed doors that actually PJ was off shopping to Bangalore on Thursday as he couldn't make it over on the Wednesday. I actually thought this was hilarious, maybe PJ had a bit of Manc 'blag' in him too :)

I do think that if you're hammering the 6 day practice rule (another bloody Ashtanga rule, I just don't like being told what to do that's my problem) to take an extra rest day (as well as Sunday) every other week makes absolute sense – just to give your body some time out from the intensity of practice. I just don't think we have to look too deeply into why we are resting and rely on some ancient Hindu scripture for Moon Day justification. I've read some of these scriptures (insert sleeping emoji) and to quote The Smiths enigmatic (and fellow cynical Mancunian) Stephen Patrick Morrissey 'it says nothing to me about my life'. I prefer a more plausible explanation a friend of mine gave me a while back. In the Hindu religion the Moon days are considered to be very auspicious and so there are extra-long 'Pujas' (religious services) on these days – no time for throwing a few shapes on a sticky blue/purple /emerald /whatever yoga mat.

So final point from me is that I think it's important to listen to our teachers and their advice, teachings, and instructions. But it's also important to have the responsibility to come to your own conclusions and act on that conclusion. So it's Full Moon today and normally I would be getting 'jiggy wit it' on me mat but as it happens I need some new jeans so I'm making like a Guru and going shopping instead. Laters.

The reports of the death of Ashtanga Yoga have been greatly exaggerated

April 2016

So I'm walking round my local neighbourhood in the Venice Beach area of LA trying to get my bearings and also get a feel for the place, and for the people, when as luck would have it I stumble across a yoga studio. Well to be honest there was no luck involved – yoga studios are two a penny here. It seems there's one literally on every street corner. Anyway I thought I'd go in, say hello, and make some 'connections' with my fellow yogis. The owner/ founder bloke was sat on his tod in reception – let's call him Dave for now. I introduced myself to ol' Dave and told him I was new to the area and that I taught Ashtanga yoga – have done for over 15 years and that I'd been to Mysore a bunch of times.

'Oh no-one is interested in Ashtanga anymore buddy,' Dave informed me. 'I mean I practice Ashtanga myself but it's all about the Vinyasa Flow now – check this out,' to which he hands me his studio's timetable. A quick scan of his timetable tells me that it IS all about the Vinyasa Flow for his studio – no shit! There were no other classes other than Vinyasa Flow on there! I wanted to make a snarky comment about him saying that he practiced Ashtanga, and how I doubted whether he could SEE his toes let alone touch them, but I held my Northern tongue and tumbled back out onto the street feeling completely bewildered, my mind all in a tiz. Has Ashtanga really bitten the dust, I thought to myself. Is it time for me to go with the (vinyasa) flow and do some new fad yoga 200 hours teacher training programme*. Have things gotten that bad that I'll have to start teaching Boxing Yoga™ ** or maybe even much, much worse... the dreaded Hot Yoga. I could see the headlines now 'Yoga teacher who never had anything good to say about Hot Yoga now teaching Hot Yoga.' I nearly collapsed at the thought.

The next day I decided I was going to 'take practice' at the local Ashtanga yoga studio up the road. Usually I just practice at home (as this means I can do it in my under pants and can break wind anytime I bloody well want to without fear of offending anyone). I'd not been to this studio before but if Vinyasa Dave was correct I guess I'd be there on my own with a couple of tumble weeds blowing round the studio. I got there nice and early and parked up the motor and then proceeded to walk into a jam packed studio full of Ashtangis – my heart leapt with joy – ok maybe that's a little poetic for a sarcastic Mancunian... let's just say I was reet happy! I felt like running round and high fiving everyone – I actually felt like taking a short video and messaging it to Vinyasa Dave with a caption saying 'Ashtanga's not dead, BUDDY' but didn't.

After class I'm driving home with that lovely post Ashtanga buzz with a big smile on my face. It's almost like smoking a medicinal herbal cigarette but without the paranoia and halitosis. I've mentioned this countless times before but to me practicing Ashtanga makes me feel great. It's a no brainer – why wouldn't anyone want to feel like this? It makes life that little bit sweeter, and easier to navigate. Yes it's hard to get up in the morning especially when it's cold, wet, and damp but boy, oh boy, oh boy it is worth it – try it for yourself. You might just start to like your boss – or at least accept his/her terrible witticisms.

So just a heads up to Vinyasa Dave: Ashtanga yoga is alive and kicking – and has been for hundreds (if not thousands) of years, my dim-witted friend. It has an ultra-rich history, heritage, and tradition that other 'Johnny come lately' yoga traditions can only dream of. (I must say it does feel good to know that this practice that I am dedicating my life to was borne out of a want to improve the self and not the self's bank balance). Ashtanga Yoga will still be going strong when you've turned your studio into a Cage-Fighting Yoga emporium or any other completely bunk form of physical practice that the money men have paired up with Yoga.

* can I just say for the record that God only knows who or what team of imbeciles/con men came up with the magic number of 200 hours as an appropriate length of time to deem someone capable and competent to teach yoga. Meh!

** if the person that teaches Boxing Yoga In Manchester is reading this please please please stop emailing me about hosting a Yoga Boxing workshop. I have no interest whatsoever about the ridiculous money making scheme of pairing yoga and boxing and even less interest in supporting a workshop. Many thanks – have a lovely day!

Before Samadhi Surya Namaskar, After Samadhi Surya Namaskar

October 2015

So the more spiritually minded folk will have spotted that I've taken a small liberty of rebranding the famous Zen quote, "Before enlightenment chop wood carry water, after enlightenment chop wood carry water," for the Yoga posse out there. But it's the same thing. Or maybe it isn't...

As Van Morrison sung, 'Enlightenment, don't know what it is.'

Neither do I, Van my friend. And neither do I know what samadhi is. And judging by the amount of folk I've met along the well-trodden dusty Avenue of Ashtanga neither does anybody else.

So what is samadhi? What is enlightenment? Do they exist? Are they like a magical place or a magical state of mind? My Zen teacher Brad Warner, who has had such an experience, insists that enlightenment is for 'sissies'.

I don't want to get too bogged down into the definition and etymologies of either samadhi or enlightenment. I'm not clever enough, for a start. But sticking to Ashtanga Yoga for now (as I know slightly more about it than I do Zen – and when I say *know* I mean you could write all of this knowledge on a postage stamp and still have room left for the shopping list) I stumbled into this practice by default rather than design and was swept along with the promise of the illusive 8th limb. Guruji would make the statement that we would have to create strong bodies before we could consider our minds and therefore we are to practice the 3rd limb of Ashtanga Yoga (asana). And then some.

So I've practiced and practiced and practiced some more. I have good days and bad with practice just like I have good days and bad days with life. When I do practice I feel better so I'm more inclined to get on my mat rather than make excuses not to. I don't even think about the 8 limbs anymore. Nor do I even think about where the practice came from. And without wanting to offend anyone – the physical practice does not come from Patanjali's Yoga Sutras. How do I know? I did the math...

And to be brutally honest, I think if you're still clinging to the belief that the practice is 5,000 years old you're missing the point. We should take a leaf out of the Buddha's book when someone asked him 'Is there a God or is there not a God?' Buddha's reply was to remain silent. The silence was a demonstration of the ridiculousness of the question.

There's a great quote from Matthew Sweeney who said the only reason that people get their knickers in a twist about the Yoga Sutras is because it has the word 'Yoga' in it (ok he probably didn't say knickers in a twist but you get my drift). Have a think about that quote for a moment... Go with this thought: Imagine if they had been called 'The Deep Absorptions of Patanjali.' Would we (we as in yoga students) have ever read the bloody thing? Methinks not. And please, please any yoga scholars/practitioners out there thinking about a new angle on a Sutra commentary, do some asana instead. Do something that you can actually experience rather than writing about something you can only intellectually understand. Put it this way: Would you trust a book about the qualities of sugar written by someone who has NEVER tasted sugar?

But if you like it? Read it, chant it – go for it! I don't have time for it personally. I think people are trying to put square pegs in round holes. In the words (or lyrics should I say) of Stephen Patrick Morrisey from the hit single 'Panic' with his beat combo The Smiths...

'It says nothing to me about my life'

What does resonate with me is when I see quotes like this one...

'When you get to the top of the mountain,keep climbing.'

Yes, I know this can be construed as another 'pithy' Zen statement. Yet when I read it my brain reinterprets this for my yoga asana sensibility as another way of saying, 'When you've done Surya Namaskar, do it again.' The samadhi is in the doing, not in the achieving. Let us not get carried away by thoughts of samadhi or indeed being enlightened. And certainly let us not get carried away by our physical prowess or gymnastic ability.

Here's yet another (pithy) Zen quote from the late great Alan Watts...

'Zen does not confuse spirituality with thinking about God while peeling potatoes. Zen is just peeling potatoes.'

I think we could rephrase that beauty to something like this...

Ashtanga Yoga is not in the pontification of the Yoga Sutras or even in the boring laborious debate about how old the practice is. Ashtanga Yoga is Ekam inhale Dve exhale. And so on...

Perhaps we can also take a leaf out the book of Dogen, the 12th century Japanese Zen Monk. Dogen basically said taking the posture of Zazen was enlightenment itself, meaning that the practice of zazen and the experience of enlightenment were one. And so maybe to take (asana) practice is samadhi.

I read somewhere that one Zen teacher on entering a Zendo (a place where people practice Zazen meditation) full of his students remarked, 'What a silly thing to do!' and then proceeded to join them. And I must say this thought (what a silly thing to do) crosses my mind a few dozen times during practice – usually in postures like Garbha Pindasana or Tittibhasana B when I'm looking up my own backside... I mean WTF? But I do it and I do it again.

So keep climbing the mountain and keep digging for that bone Yoga warriors... Samadhi is for wussies

Ashtanga Yoga – A personal statement.

July 2019

More allegations, more confusion, more mudslinging... Teachers revising opinions, teachers hiding opinions, teachers refusing to have an opinion. After the recent Instagram post by Sharath Jois, there is now no debate as to the guilt of Pattabhi Jois and the many allegations against him of sexually assaulting women under the guise of adjustments. Anyone who wants to continue to deny these allegations are either stupid or complicit or both.

As an Ashtanga teacher I've personally had to have a very long and hard look at myself recently and one thing that I do know is that I've never needed to have any connection to the practice via anyone other than myself. So the way that manifests when I'm teaching is comparable to the parable of the raft in the Buddhist tradition....

A man travelling along a path came to a great expanse of water. As he stood on the shore, he realised there were dangers and discomforts all about. But the other shore appeared safe and inviting. The man looked for a boat or a bridge and found neither. But with great effort he gathered grass, twigs, and branches and tied them all together to make a simple raft. Relying on the raft to keep himself afloat, the man paddled with his hands and feet and reached the safety of the other shore. He could continue his journey on dry land.

Now, what would he do with his makeshift raft? Would he drag it along with him or leave it behind? He would leave it, the Buddha said. Then the Buddha explained that the dharma is like a raft: It is useful for crossing over but not for holding onto.

I hope I don't have to flesh this out too much for folk to get my drift. Students come to class and need guidance from me. And although I've been practising Ashtanga for 20 plus years, I wouldn't say I'm any kind of authority whatsoever. But I've embraced the practice and feel I'm well placed to pass on what I've learned that is specific to the students' individual needs. I'm there at class as myself (and I'm not representing anyone other than myself or any allegiance to any particular part of the various Ashtanga traditions and its numerous contradictions) I'm helping them by teaching what I know only. The more enthusiastic students will pick up what I'm teaching them more quickly and won't need me as much, others might need more input from me for a longer period of time. The idea is that I've managed to help them get from A to B in the practice – from a place of a beginner to a position where they feel comfortable knowing what they are doing. As in the parable above I'm acting like a raft to the student – they need me for a specific time only – and as just mentioned that specific time is unique for every individual in class. Once the student gets to B I'm happy for them to tie me up by the side of the stream and get back on whenever they need to. They don't have to (nor will I let them) put me on any kind of a pedestal for helping them out.

A good western analogy is in the Football (soccer) Coach. So a good coach like Pep Guardiola has the ability to treat each member of the team as an individual, e.g some players need a bit of TLC , enthusiastic but gentle vocal encouragement to help support and get the best out of them, while other players respond better to loud, vocal, motivational instructions (like move yer arse you lazy bugger!). And as an ex-football manager (well ok I managed my son's under 8 football team to a league and cup double one season and then quit straight after – leave on a high note!) I think this is a good analogy to make. Although I've never yet met a yoga student who responded well to me shouting at them to get their arses in gear .

Ashtanga Yoga (i.e. the practice, the teachers, and the way it is taught) is currently going through a much needed period of transformation. A very good friend of mine and another Ashtanga Yoga teacher Luke Jordan said 'we are all responsible for ourselves, to do the right thing in each moment.' For all its faults I think social media can help the community of Ashtanga Yoga by bringing the problems of the practice to light, and to help find the solutions to move it forward, while also making sure this type of thing never happens again. At the very least it can start the conversation.

I first went to Mysore in January 2000 – the classes were still held in the tiny old 12 students at a time Shala. It was a very intimate experience and perhaps even a little intimidating – especially for myself. I felt somewhat (and still do tbh) like a fish out of water. I had started Ashtanga Yoga maybe 12 months previous to that first trip to help combat an extreme anxiety disorder I had. I wasn't looking for any kind of spiritual guidance or awakening. I am fortunate that I have four older sisters (me being the youngest and only boy) and have a very strong matriarchal mindset, and so when all the other students at the Shala would refer to Pattabhi Jois as 1. An Enlightened Being (whatever that means) and 2. Guruji, I was highly sceptical. I think my Mancunian upbringing gave me for better or worse a rather cynical outlook, so I was (and still to this day) remain suspicious of anyone calling themselves a Guru. I never really felt any kind of connection and still don't to the *spiritual aspect* of Ashtanga Yoga and the links to the Hindu religion. I'm happy that some Yoga students can make sense of the Yoga Sutras of Patanjali. Myself? I personally feel it's a rather dense esoteric meditation manual that's got naff all to do with the physical asana practice. I mean who needs to be told it's wrong to steal, to not tell the truth, etc. in the 21st century by an (allegedly) second century textbook (Oh! cynical me).

I wasn't aware of any wrong doings by Pattabhi Jois until a few years after my first visit when mutterings had gone around Mysore about his 'inappropriate adjustments' and to be honest he'd stopped teaching by then so I guess it was a case of out of sight out of mind. Then the Internet happened (albeit on a much smaller scale than it is today) and the photo evidence started appearing. He passed away in 2009 and to a certain extent as far as I was aware the above mutterings stopped. I must state also as mentioned above I always felt like a fish out of water when I was in Mysore. I was never in with the in-crowd. I was never *in the loop* with the comings and goings of Mysore. I spent most of my time hanging out with the kids from Operation-Shanti, the charity I am an ambassador for.

The #metoo campaign of the last few years, particular the heart wrenching testimony of Karen Rain, brought to light the reality of Pattabhi Jois's reprehensible behaviour. There have been multiple testimonies since Karen Rain's initial statement (there have also been plenty of articles in the Yoga Journal, Elephant Journal, petitions on change.org, students writing open letters, rescinding their authorization and certification, and so on). One certified teacher has stopped practising altogether and closed her Ashtanga studio down for good.

I am not in any position to advise others what they should or shouldn't do – to stop practicing or to keep practicing. My connection to Ashtanga never was (or is) via anything other than a commitment to my own mental & physical well-being, which there is no doubt at all the practise has helped considerably. All I'm doing when I'm teaching is to just try and be the best teacher I can be for the student on the day – it's that simple.

*A few hours later I read and reread the above several times. It's imperfect and I apologise for that. But I've done my best and I wanted to try and find the right words to show my respect to all those students who have been affected by all of this.

The Yoga Revolution will be Live (online via Zoom)

May 2020

Well who would have thunk it. If you'd have said to me three or four months back (when actually did lock down begin – it seems like forever ago) that I'd be teaching yoga folk around the world via my iPhone I would have prolly questioned your marbles – equally if you (you being the all-seeing you!) would have told the majority of yoga students around the world that they would be taking their yoga classes in the near future via their smart phones/tablets/laptops, they too would have said (assume your best Glaswegian accent) 'yer off ya hed wee man!' But hey hey hey, here we all are, and now after busting an iPhone yoga teaching tail feather since the start of lockdown and after a little bit of reluctance on my part to begin with, I must say that I'm now enjoying this new yoga teaching ride!

The lock down for me – like a lot of people – was pretty stressful if I'm being honest. We were living in a shoe box in Venice Beach, Los Angeles - oh first world problems I hear you cry, and yes there is a bit of that I'm sorry, but it was still pretty brutal. We being my wife, my two kids (Boo, daughter aged 6, and Easy, son aged 3) and myself. Prior to lockdown Boo my daughter would get dropped at school at 8am in the morning and then picked up at 6pm – 3 hours of free after school club (yes you heard that right – free as in we didn't have to pay) - even at 6pm you'd have to pry her off the climbing frame to get her home. Easy would be in nursery 8am-4pm – so both out of the house most of the day Mon-Fri – so in the blink of an eye they both went from this to being cooped up in our tiny space with their wonderful fabulous Mother and their grumpy short tempered Father (ok I'm not that bad!). Parks, beaches, public spaces all closed – thank goodness we had a tiny backyard to swing a cat in. I spent most of my mornings digging for worms with Easy - using kitchen utensils - at the back of the apartment in the communal gardens – god only knows what the neighbours thought of us – weird English family probably.

So at the very real danger of turning into Jack Torrance, Lina, my wife, suggested to me that I should teach some yoga classes via Zoom – the only Zoom that I knew of had involved Fat Larry's Band. I had a quick butchers online to see what other teachers were up to and it became fairly obvious straight away that online video conferencing (ie Zoom) was the way forward. I decided I would do the sessions at 11 am LA time – which would be 7pm UK time thus being able to allow my US and UK students to virtually attend the sessions. And within the space of a few very, very long days I was up and running throwing shapes at my iPhone which I'd attached to a chair at the other side of the room – the worms of Venice Beach were saved! The very first session was a bit of a disaster – as soon as I made the decision to start the classes, the Matt Ryan PR department (ie *moi*) went into hyper drive and made all the right social media song & dance noises plus I had decided to do the classes for free to begin with as I was aware loads of folk were off work and not getting paid. So day 1 turned into a bit of a bun fight as literally as soon as the session had begun I started getting a load of text messages/emails, etc from angry students who hadn't been able to access the inaugural session. It soon became apparent that I'd exceeded the 100 person limit of the 'video conference' and I'd now got a bunch of angry students banging on the virtual shala door. What made things even worse was I'd not done my Zoom due diligence and hadn't figured out how to mute all the 100 very lucky folks who had managed to access the class. Cue all kinds of weird and wonderful 'crowd' noises from every Tom Dick & Deidre on the session, from a polite clearing of the nasal passages to the rumble explosions from 'other' bodily passages – to muffled laughter from people (myself included) – someone farting in a yoga class, even in a virtual one, will never stop being funny.

Within 24 hours I'd had a quick Zoom tutorial which showed me the all-important 'mute all' button and we were back with a bang for day 2. I'd noticed that numbers had dropped off a little from Day 1 – some people just aint got no sense of yoga wind humour. Maybe I'd also lost a few folk who didn't like my lack of yoga patter when I'm teaching! Lord shoot me down if I ever start asking students to 'picture your neck curving over a giant cloud of kittens meowing softly into a bed of dreams while licking dandelions and holding tenderly a basket of pussywillows...'

So here we all are 4 months into the Matt Ryan Yoga Zoom experience – it's been one hell of a journey and feedback has been so good that I'll continue until people stop tuning in. Classes are Mon-Fri with something different going on each night. I've just introduced my

Ashtanga Yoga Second Series Short Forms which I'm like totally blissed out about 😌 – blowing out of the water the rather ridiculous notion that (Ashtanga) yoga students have to have completed primary series before moving on to second series.

The Power of Nowt

October 2016

Ok, I'll 'fess up here. I've written about this subject many times before. But it's a theme that crops up again and again in both my yoga & meditation practices. My crazy Zen teacher Brad Warner wrote about it very eloquently in a recent blog post which made me want to reiterate the point, more for myself than anyone else. I guess the 'theme' can be boiled down to one word: Expectations.

What is the criteria that fulfils our expectations from practice? Be it to become strong, fit, and flexible from yoga asana or perhaps we use meditation to become more mindful, chilled out, or even to achieve enlightenment (whatever the hell that is), we all start or continue with these disciplines for a reason. My own reasons for starting yoga (and meditation) were all mind based but I did have expectations that these practices were going to 'fix' my mind. And just for the record here I continue to have expectations as much as the next person.

But as I mentioned in a previous blog: What the hell happens when your practices aint ticking your expectation boxes? Where do you go from there? Do you pack it in? Do you keep going until your donkey & carrot expectations are fulfilled in a never ending chasing your tail 'kinda way?

I guess for myself I only truly understood about expectations when I started to do this Zazen thang (Zazen is the 'Zen' Buddhist form of meditation). There are actually a few different methods of 'Zazen', and the one I practice is called shikantaza (pronounced she-can-tar-za) which literally means 'just sitting'. In shikantaza all we are doing is just sitting up straight on a 'zafu' (meditation cushion) in full lotus, half-lotus or with cross legs, with eyes open, looking at a wall (I'll elaborate the wall thing in another blog). So there's no counting breaths or reciting mantras or any other similar methods that one would do in other meditation practices. When one does shikantaza you're not trying to get anywhere or achieve anything which is probably the complete antithesis of everything you've been taught and begs the question 'why on earth would you want to sit and stare at a wall for 40 minutes a day if it's not actually doing anything?' And believe you me that particular question does crop up a bazillion times when I'm sitting. When I ask Brad how to deal with this endless questioning by my mind his answer is always the same. 'Just sit Matt,' he says. 'Ah ok, thanks,' I would reply. End of lesson. Just sit!

Now in Yoga asana there are obvious tangible benefits when you start practicing. After a while maybe you can touch your toes (or even see your toes), your shoulders and hips feel looser and usually there is a general feeling of well-being after your yoga practice. But in my own experience these benefits start to become less obvious after a while, I mean I'm fairly flexible now and there's a chunk of yoga postures in the Ashtanga practice that I can't do and probably never will be able to. And sometimes my mind is as messy as it was before I had practiced that day. So rather than beat myself up about it I heed Brad's words about sitting and apply it to yoga – I just practice. There's something very powerful in the ability to do something 'just for the sake of doing it,' to achieve nothing in particular, without any grand mental or physical expectations. Nothing (or the Northern colloquialism 'Nowt') is where it's at, man!

There is a fly in this expectation-less ointment though. How can you stop the mind expecting? And here's the secret answer that I am giving you for FREE that other Yoga/ Meditation snake charmers might charge you the earth for. You can't. Really it's that simple. As I mentioned before your mind literally has a mind of its own. Its job *is* to think. What it thinks you have absolutely no control over whatsoever and therein lies the problem. We think we can control the mind but the reality is we can't – so why bother trying! What we can do is not react to the endless cycle of mundane incessant questions the mind conjures up. My body is still stiff and I've been practicing yoga for five and a half weeks now, I can't get my leg(s) behind my head, my practice doesn't feel as good as it did last week, and on and on it goes. So rather than have answers for these questions or even trying to fulfill the expectations you just carry on with practice and accept that it's just the mind carrying on with itself. As Brad says, 'A big part of doing shikantaza practice is learning how to be OK with your thoughts being completely out of control.' And it's the same with yoga asana too. Both these practices for me are the same thing – as Yoga teacher David Williams says 'Yoga & Meditation are synonyms.'

So next time you come to one of my classes and you ask me why you can't get your leg behind your head or why you can't touch your toes I'll most likely tell you to not worry too much and 'just practice'.

The Second Noble Truth: Life (with kids) is suffering.

February 2020

It has been said that parenting is the actual Seventh Series of Ashtanga Yoga, but whoever came up with that phrase obviously hasn't met my kids. My kids bypassed the seventh series – the eighth and the ninth, too, for that matter. Parenting my kids is a double figures type of practice, or to quote Morrissey, 'November spawned a monster'!

For those who didn't have the pleasure of reading about my last single parenting journey to the apocalypse, please fill your boots and check the *Shit Happens* chapter. Oh Joy.

So when I said I'd quit single parenting travel after the aforementioned Armageddon shit show, what I actually meant to say was I'd quit travelling alone with my son Easy - my mind, body, and soul simply could not be dragged through that particular experience ever again. But travelling alone with Boo, my bright and bubbly 6 year old, well that'd be a breeze surely? Well surely not as it happens …

Yet another school holiday provided me with an opportunity of nipping back to Blighty (with Boo) to catch up with friends and family and remind myself of the incredible climate that Manchester can boast of (incredible in that it can rain, snow, sleet, rain more, be colder than the Antarctic, sideways rain, have a glimpse of sun before, yes, more rain, and all in just one day). The air fare for 1 adult and 1 child was actually cheaper than the racket of winter camp LA – go figure.

We arrived at LAX with probably too much time to spare but I thought this would be a great opportunity to read my book whilst Boo harassed other kids into playing with her at the play area at the airport. Big fat fail – either the Child Catcher from Chitty Chitty Bang Bang had been doing overtime or all the parents had spotted Boo arriving and hid in the toilets with their kids. She has a reputation, you know. So I had two choices: get involved in Boo's psychotic hide n' seek/tag games or the usual parenting 'go to' in these circumstances... buy her off. Yes, of course, I chose the latter. And Boo's buying off tipple of choice is candy (or sweets for my UK brothers and sisters). After spending what seemed like a *trouser pulling down* amount of money on three separate items of candy we headed for the flight.

Yes I know what you're thinking here … 'ooh Matt you've given your daughter a bunch of candy right before an eleven hour flight, that's gonna come back to bite you on the ass.' In just under an hour of being airborne, buying my daughter three bags of candy came back to bite me on the ass. It had all been going so well. In fact, there are distinct similarities between the start of this flight with Boo and the other one with Easy – perhaps they were in collusion with each other, and to be frank I wouldn't put it past them. So the candy had the opposite effect of what it normally does to Boo, i.e. normally she'd be bouncing off the seats and around the aisles whilst I'd be pretending to be asleep pretending she wasn't my daughter, but after scoffing down the LOT on take-off she promptly fell asleep. Ah, happy days. I could finally settle down with my book. Was it page four or five I had gotten to when Boo's deep aero slumber came to a rather ass biting end as she stirred with the murmur of, 'Daddy I feel sick.' I pretended not to hear. Yes, she must be talking in her sleep. I prayed to any particular God who might be listening – given I was in their neighbourhood you would have thought they might have helped me out here?

And then it happened.

In the time one could say, "Get the sick bag out of the seat pocket in front of you," Boo had gone from *Daddy I feel sick* to *Daddy I'm going to be sick* to actually sitting bolt upright and puking her little guts out into the cupping of my hands. I was actually quite proud of myself that I had managed to drop my book and cup my hands underneath her mouth in no less than 3 nano seconds – maybe I was a cowboy in a previous life. We both looked down into the marinated candy infused barf that was swilling around my hand bowl. Well, things could be worse, I thought.

And then things actually did get worse. Boo coughed and then heaved a second honk helping on top of the first taking the total portion to the very edge of both my nerves and the rim of the hand-bowl. Boo blinked, looked at me, then at my hands, then lay down and fell fast asleep. We were sat in two of three seats, Boo next to the window, me in the middle and Mr Smelly Fart, a portly gentleman who was sat slumped snoring like a chainsaw in the seat next to the aisle.

So WTF am I going to do now? I considered my options. I was hardly gonna try and step over Mr SF and make my way to the bathroom. Even figuring that out in my mind gave me a headache as that was a plan destined to end in tears with me tripping and spilling. I know! I'll call a flight attendant who can bring me a XL sick bag and help clean this mess up. But Matt, again I hear you say, how on earth can you press the button to call said flight attendant with your hands full of kiddie stinking vomit? (Which was now mixing it up with the aroma from Mr Smelly Fart's backside and making me feel like I was gonna gip myself any minute.) Well my friends, this is where my 20+ years of yoga practice was finally going to pay off. I precariously balanced the contents of Boo's chunder (does this blog hold the record for sick euphemisms?) above my head and whilst sticking my cranium between my arms proceeded to press the smallest on screen 'call flight attendant' button WITH MY NOSE! Yes folks, I kid you not. Just picture that if you can – Matt Ryan, advanced yoga teacher, using his physiological dexterity to press a button on a small aeroplane seat screen with his nose. But of course that didn't work – it seems these buttons are touch sensitive with fingers only – how noseist can you get! It was now obvious to me that 'someone up there,' well 'up here,' didn't like me very much, and considering the emotional and mental scars created by Easy's shit show on the last flight one could safely assume that I wasn't going to heaven.

Thinking on my feet, or *with* my feet, I kicked all the contents of the foot well underneath the seat in front of me and threw Boo's business (eye rolling emoji) on the floor. What else could I do? I covered the mess with a couple of sick bags, wiped my hands clean, and proceeded to update my wonderful wife on how the journey was going so far with a WhatsApp message (caps lock on). There's nothing that says you are royally pissed off more than a caps lock on WhatsApp message.

Me: I CAN'T BELIEVE THIS IS FXXKING HAPPENING AGAIN

Wife: What's happened now?

Me: YOUR* FXXKING DAUGHTER HAS JUST PUKED EVERYWHERE

(Why is it that parents always refer to their children as belonging to their spouse when the child has done something wrong?)

Wife: Oh no, is she sick? Does she have a fever?

Me: NO SHE ATE A BUNCH OF CANDY BEFORE THE FLIGHT

Wife: Right, I think there's a little moral to this story, Matthew.

Me: AAAAAARRRRGGGHHHHHHHHHHHHHH

So a word of advice to all you budding yoga enthusiasts: Yoga will help make you become more flexible and strong. It might even help you to press an on flight monitor screen with your nose. But it probably won't help you from losing your shit when you fly solo with your kids.

The Magical Tale of Ernest Yogi & the Magic Lamp

August 2015

Once upon a time in the northwest of Somewhere there was a young man called Ernest Yogi. And despite Ernest having the world at his feet, he would walk around town with a permanent rain cloud above his head. He felt that he had more problems than anyone else in the world.

One day whilst pounding the pavements of Ancoats on the way to a yoga class, he chanced upon a very beautiful golden lamp...a Magic Lamp no less. (Ok you'll need to suspend your disbelief here about the chance of finding a magic lamp on a pavement in Ancoats, but for the sake of the story just go with the flow.) Our young depressed hero picked the lamp up and gave it a bit of a wipe, as it was covered in cigarette butts and car oil. And then *KERPOW*! out popped Patanjali, the Genie of the Magic Lamp. Young Ernest staggered back and had to pinch himself to make sure this was all really happening and not the after effects of his medicinal 'herbal' cigarettes.

'I can grant you one wish and one wish only,' Patanjali said to Ernest.

'Oh thank-you Mr. Genie, could you please, please get rid of all my problems,' came Ernest's reply.

Patanjali the Genie raised an eyebrow and spoke, 'Are you sure you don't want a million pounds or a big mansion or perhaps a decent leg behind head?'

Patanjali knew that young Ernest was struggling with lots of things, including poor hip flexors on the right side.

'It's tempting to go for a decent leg behind head, but I just want all my problems to be gone.' Ernest was firm with what he thought would make him happiest.

'So be it,' Patanjali said. 'I want you to find a big box and put all your problems in it and then meet me here at the same time tomorrow'.

(More suspension of disbelief necessary here about being able to put problems in a box - Cheers.)

The next day Ernest Yogi arrived at the very same spot that Patanjali the Genie had appeared. He had with him a massive box (the big wooden ones that you get from Unicorn in Chorlton) with all his problems inside. *KERPOW!* Patanjali appeared once more out of the Magic Lamp and spoke to Ernest,

'Ok sunny Jim, follow me and let's see if we can sort out the problem with your problems.'

Ernest Yogi set off behind the Genie down the back streets of Ancoats. After five minutes of dodging crazy barking stray dogs and strange gaunt looking men asking to lend 50 pence for their 'bus fare,' they arrived at a big warehouse – a warehouse big enough to fit in boxes of problems from everyone in the whole world.

'Ok Ernest Yogi, inside this big warehouse is boxes of problems from everyone in the whole world. You have exactly one hour to go inside and swap your box of problems for someone else's.'

'YES!' shrieked Ernest. 'That's absolutely brilliant, I'll just go find David Beckham's box or maybe even The Dalai Lamas, they'll both be bloody empty!' And off he went into the warehouse.

Patanjali waited patiently outside. Within only a few minutes the door burst open and our unhappy hero came scurrying out, carrying the very same box that he went in with, and shouting, 'No way, no way, I'll keep my own box of problems thanks very much!'

And off he went into the sunset with his own big box of problems, perhaps not weighing as heavy on his mind as he once thought.

'Ah,' sighed Patanjali. 'That one works every time!'

The End.

Me dad (RIP) told me that story years and years ago, before I even started Yoga. The hero in his story wasn't called Ernest Yogi and neither was the genie called Patanjali, but apart from that it's pretty much the same way he used to tell it. Quite recently I passed it on to my own son.

Of course it's a very simple story straight out of kindergarten, but that doesn't lessen the power of the message. It's hard to see the way out sometimes when we are stuck in a dark space. There's a brilliant Eckhart Tolle quote from his *The Power of Now* book. He says something along the lines of, 'Sometimes there doesn't seem to be a way out, but there's always a way through.' How pretty feckin' radical is that – there's always a way through. It's so easy to think that people like the Dalai Lama and Posh n' Becks don't have any problems. But of course – we ALL have problems. Every single one of us. The problems are not so much the problem, but how we deal with them.

So the above fable is perhaps only half the story. We can acknowledge we are not alone in having problems and we can find some solace in that fact but what next? This is where my yoga practice comes in. There's some amazing health benefits to be had from taking a regular yoga practice (including a strong fit flexible body) but for me it's the mental health benefits I'm after baby! Yes, life is tough and I've got a ton of problems (who hasn't?) but I do my practice and though the problems don't exactly disappear, their firm grip on my mind becomes more like a gentle squeeze.

Guru is not Great *

December 2019

I was listening to a podcast recently where a meditating neuroscientist called Sam Harris was interviewing the infamous cult leader/spiritual teacher Andrew Cohen. SH was taking AC to task over his creation of basically a cult disguised as a spiritual community, and the mental (and physical) chaos his teachings (teachings that he would refer to as crazy wisdom) had caused his followers. It was a fascinating listen – but my main take away from it was near the end of the conversation when SH asks AC if the idea of the Eastern Guru in the context of the modern world is now both broken and unsalvageable, with AC agreeing.

I wrote recently about the big black dark cloud hanging over Ashtanga yoga in light of the allegations of sexual abuse against Pattabhi Jois – the guru of Ashtanga yoga. It seems this dark cloud is nowhere near finding any light of resolution as more allegations of abuse and senior teacher cover-ups continue to come out in the public sphere (mainly via social media). Having been to Mysore numerous times I do admit I drank the Kool Aid along with everybody else, but if I'm honest with myself I spat it out when no-one was watching. It felt weird (and still does) that people would need to elevate another person into a Guru – an ideal being. I didn't understand it. I'm of course not saying it's wrong, obvs, I'm just saying it's not for me. I've been studying Zen meditation for the last 10 years or so now, and one of the biggest lessons for me in this tradition is that any Zen student trying to give their responsibility away to the Zen Master – a responsibility that says 'please show me how to live my life' gets thrown right back at them and the admonishment 'take responsibility for yourself'! I think it's time for Ashtanga to learn this lesson. I don't know what it is about Ashtanga but some of its teachers love to have the power of this responsibility - they want to become the Guru themselves instead of wanting to awaken the Guru in the student. A word of advice here to students, any teacher/Guru/Paramaguru (sigh) teaching 'it's my way or the highway' – choose the highway every time. And by 'my way' they usually mean 'the traditional method' – it's pretty ironic (and tragic) that there are countless teachers teaching contradictory 'traditional methods.' As my good friend Luke Jordan says, 'Let's be done with the silly insistence on a militaristic, mythological *correct method*."

I can also admit now for the first time to anyone who is vaguely interested that after quitting last Summer a Mysore programme I was teaching in Los Angeles (because of the aforementioned black cloud) I was seriously considering packing in teaching altogether- I know some teachers already had. One teacher wrote that they felt Pattabhi Jois and

Ashtanga yoga were synonymous so this person could no longer in good faith practice or teach Ashtanga yoga. I have never felt this way – personally I always attributed the Ashtanga practice and sequences to Krishnamacharya (Pattabhi Jois's teacher). I have some copies of Krishnamacharya Yoga Mandiram darsanam : a quarterly publication from the Krishnamacharya Yoga Mandiram. There are various photo essays in these magazines showing students moving through what was called Vinayasa Krama sequences that Krishnamacharya had created. To me these sequences are almost a carbon copy of the (mainly primary series) Ashtanga sequences – coincidence? Me thinks not. There are also YouTube videos of a young BKS Iyengar moving through parts of the advanced Ashtanga sequences in the early 1930s and we know who his teacher was. I will add a small caveat to this point by admitting that apart from some written testimonies from his students we don't really know what kind of teacher Krishnamacharya really was. There are reports that he regularly hit and chastised students and by giving him the honour of the Ashtanga creator I might also be swapping one feet of clay for another. I digress.

What pulled me round and back onto the mat and into the classroom was the inspiration I found via student testimonials I had received. They literally brought tears to my eyes. They brought the comfort of knowing that despite everything I was of some value to a few people, and that's good enough for me. And after 20 plus years of both teaching and practicing I don't need anyone else's approval. I don't feel I have to justify myself for wanting to teach Ashtanga Yoga in a non-traditional and secular way. As I mentioned in a previous blog, I don't need to connect to Ashtanga either when I'm teaching or practicing via a third party (Mysore/ Pattabhis Jois / Sharath etc) – I connect to students via my own experience, the 20 years plus of blood, sweat, and tears that I've put into it. Peace Out/Off.

Afterword

I was listening to a discussion via YouTube between LA recording artist Earl Sweatshirt and his mother Professor Cheryl Harris. PCH was telling a story that a couple of years back after the terrible news of the Donald, ES had asked her if America could be fixed. She was heartbroken to say no it couldn't but something new had to be built. Personally I think this is analogous to Ashtanga yoga – it is broken beyond repair in its present guise and it needs to be rebuilt. This rebuilding process will need intelligence and compassion for the student and making sure their internal/external needs are of paramount importance, and the adherence to some bogus idea of sticking to a militaristic mythological 'correct method' should be left in the rubble.

A very good friend of mine and a senior Ashtanga teacher told me a true story of how many moons ago he had joined the Hare Krishna movement, as he saw this as a real opportunity of furthering his spiritual understanding and practice. After a few months or so he noticed that the students who were becoming more 'spirituality advanced' as decided by the Hare Krishna hierarchy, were actually the students who were selling the most books on the street. He left the movement. I can see similarities with Ashtanga Yoga here where flexibility is rewarded with status – how spiritual, eh! For me there is nothing spiritual at all about a sequence of physical movements that help to increase one's strength and flexibility. The only thing spiritual is the person doing the movements.

* Thanks to the late Christopher Hitchens for the inspiration for the blog title.

Mysore (Ass) Part 1

June 2009

Mysore is the birthplace of Ashtanga yoga. As a reference point it's a couple of centimetres below Bangalore on a map of South India - and if you don't know where Bangalore is I'm sorry I can't help you. Try Mahatma Google...

If you've never been to India, no amount of me trying to describe the insanity that passes for everyday normal life there is going to help. Book a ticket and go find out for yourself. Watch out for the cows and the traffic. I could write a whole chapter on Indian traffic - but to be as brief as possible, imagine that every single person that gets behind a steering mechanism has also signed up for suicide watch - and I say person as in man, woman, child, whatever, I think part of their driving criteria is based on if can you touch the peddles or not. So get out of the way - they won't stop. They don't have the pedestrian right of way laws there. In fact, they don't actually have any laws there. Traffic police are only employed to extort money from you if they manage to pull you over for any old trumped up reason.

It's a thing there to carry as much luggage as possible, especially if you are travelling by motorbike. And the luggage can be people or chickens or electric goods. In fact you're just as likely to die from a telly falling on your head as you are from being knocked over. My advice? Stick to the side of the roads - I would say footpath but that would be an exaggeration - just look for the part of the road that has the most shit on it - and I mean shit as in cow dung - the cow dung breaks up the rest of muck folk have chucked on the floor. You name it, it's on the roadside in India. Empty bottles, half a pair of jeans (praps the poor bugger only had one leg?), a toilet (a symbol, maybe!). As well as an absence of proper footpaths there's an absence of trash cans.

Right, that's the traffic situation cleared up.

As a shit kicker scally from Manchester I wasn't prepared for any of the above. I'd been practicing Ashtanga Yoga for maybe six months when I made the decision to go to the source and pay my respeck init to the teachers. I had a bit of a reputation with my mates as someone who didn't stick at things for long and the fact I was prepared to travel halfway round the world to practice yoga was my way of proving them wrong.

Me mates - Yoga? Fuks Yoga ya dickhead, and where the fuk is Indya?

Me - Knobhead

I'd done a little bit of research on t'internet, but remember folks, this was the year 2000 and there was no Trip Advisor or Google Reviews on the OG Shala. I could make summat up here about having this calling to find myself, but I'd be lying. I went because I thought it was the best way possible to understand the practice properly. Going to classes in the local school halls was great but I had this feeling that I was only skimming the surface - as a Pisces I'm an all or nutin' kinda guy - and I was all in for Ashtanga . And all in meant I knew I had to go to get my melon well and truly twisted big time in the land of soiled streets and t.v's on motorbikes.

January 2001 I landed at Bangalore Airport. The Air India flight took about a week or felt like it - it was definitely the longest I'd ever spent in an airplane. It's not that I'm a nervous flyer, more like a nervous taker-off and lander. The bit in the air I find boring. But the silver lining was that this was Air India and on Air India the boredom was punctuated with Curry meals. So not all bad. I was sat next to some Indian bloke who couldn't believe I was going to his country to study Yoga.

Indian Bloke - You are going where to study what hahahahahahahaha - nobody does yoga my friend, you need to focus on computers and technology

Me - Well as long as your country doesn't smell like your breath I'll be ok.

Ok I didn't say that - but his breath stunk and he spent the whole flight laughing in my face every ten minutes or so, incredulous that this skinny white dude was going to do yoga in India.

And then I got to India and getting off the plane onto the tarmac I was hit with this vile stench that was far worse than my neighbours gob. Oh the irony.

Me (thinking I was saying this quietly but I'd actually said it out loud) - What the fuck is that smell?

My neighbour (who was now walking with me - still mocking my plan of yoga study) Ah, that my friend is the aroma of India.

Once I'd navigated the insanity that passes for passport control I was thrown into the lion's mouth of Arrivals. Fuck me, I nearly turned round and went straight for departures. It felt like the whole of India had decided to turn up at the airport to greet me - well hardly greet, more like scream in my face. A rousing chant of TAXI TAXI COFFEE CHAI CHAI COFFEE hit me like a bastard of a drum n bass tune. Imagine being in the Hacienda on a Friday night in '89 when everyone is on one and smiling at you wanting to hold your hand - well it was a bit like that except here everyone wanted to bypass your hand and get their hands on the filthy lucre they knew you had stashed somewhere. I had the foresight to book a taxi in advance - scrub that, the travel company I booked the flight with had told me it would be a good idea to book a taxi in advance through them. And in that moment of me thinking 'fuck this I'm leaving" I spotted that beautiful shining beacon of light, a diamond, barely visible - a sign with *TAXI for Mister Maffeww Rayn* written on it. I could've kissed the taxi driver.

We fought our way to his car, me still fending off other drivers wanting my business with a very cheap deal. I'd been told that it was just a short trip from Bangalore to Mysore. Lying bastards - it was the worst three hours of my life (please read the intro again if unsure why). All I could think about when I was sat in the back of the taxi with eyes closed and fists clenched was what my mates back in Manchester were going to say at my funeral.

Mate A - Stoopid ponce. Told him Indya was a bad idea.

Mate B - he still owes me 20 quid for that E - d'u fink it'd be ok to ask his mam for it?

The car stopped. I prayed to whoever was taking prayers. I didn't know the names of the Yoga Gods (and still don't to be honest - well not all of them). I just said thank you Yoga Gods for getting me to Mysore without dying. I looked out the window to complete darkness - hhhhmmmm Mysore looks a bit gloomy - does no-one have electric here? On closer inspection all I could actually see was fields. I got out of the car and nearly fell over. The taxi driver who was taking a piss by the side of the road.

Me - Is this Mysore

Driver - oh no sorry Sir 2 more hours to go.

I think these days the road between Bangalore and Mysore have been properly tarmac'ed but back then it was basically 100 miles of pot holes, cows crossing, and enormous lorries sounding their horns to tell you to get the fuck out of their way. No wonder they have so many gods - there's a whole lot of shit you need to be saved from. If the lorries don't get you, the local water will. Even the bottled water is dangerous.

Finally we arrived in Mysore at dawn. I was delirious from a mixture of no sleep and the taxi journey. The driver wished me well and drove off. I stood motionless for maybe five minutes thinking about my journey back to the airport. I'm getting the fucking train I mumbled to myself.

I was due to stay in Mysore for a total of two months which is a whole lot longer than the two weeks I had spent on me jollies on previous trips abroad. This was definitely no jolly though and for the first two weeks my bag stayed packed.

Ozzy

June 2019

Celebrities, who are all alphabetised these days, play a big part in the Yoga Teacher's CV. The nearer to the letter A your celebrity student is, the more dollar you're gonna earn. In the past I've often been referred to as 'Yoga teacher to the Stars.' Ok, I've only ever been called that in the local paper when I was living in Manchester - so hardly Vogue Magazine. The Manchester local press idea of a star is someone off Corrie or the now deceased Brookie - both terrible and both full of actors from what we can call the celebrity C-or maybe even D list, i.e. not really a star but god luv' em they're on telly so that by default gets them on the list albeit at the lower end.

So when you get the call from Ozzy Osbourne's PA to teach yoga to the The King of Darkness, The Biter of Bats, the Heavy Metal Maniac himself, it means one of 2 things.

1: It's me daft mate taking the piss, still thinking that even though I've been teaching yoga for 20 odd years that I'm gonna one day wake up and go back on an E bender with him.

2: That thank fuck for that, after what seems like a lifetime of teaching failed actors, ie the aforementioned soap stars, I'm finally dining at the top table of A list celebrities. Maybe we could consider Ozzy to be AA - and there's a shit dad joke in there somewhere.

And thank the Lord/Buddha/Krishna/etc. that the above call was not from Madfrit Mark of Manchester. Ok I totally made that name up to get some M alliteration vibz going. Sorry I'll finish that sentence in a moment but just going off piste a little - no Mark not 'off on the piss' but off piste meaning I'm just moving away from what I was talking about. When I first emailed a piece of writing I'd done to a friend of mine in the US - let's just call him Chandler, ok that's actually his real name, I mean who the fuck would make up a name like Chandler to hide someone's identity. I mean it's a pretty embarrassing name to begin with. But anyway, he sent back a message saying that he loved it and if he was my publisher he would market me as Hunter S. Thompson in a tracksuit. Now I love Hunter. I've read most of his books and there's this weird connection between us in that he shot himself dead on 20th February which also happens to be my birthday. If you've read any of his books (his most well-known book Fear and Loathing in Las Vegas was made into a shit film with Johnny 'Dickhead' Depp) (Luv ya Johnny) you'll know that he's a brilliant writer and the high school drivel that I come out with bears absolutely no resemblance to his sharp erudite prose. With or without a tracksuit. And yes I had to look up the meaning of erudite.

Now briefly to go off-off piste: When I was diagnosed with ADHD a few years back, I very tentatively told only a few friends. Literally every one of them to a man and woman came back with 'oh I thought you already knew!' Bastards. I mean why the fuck did they keep the fact that they knew I couldn't concentrate on one thing for more than 30 seconds or even close the fucking fridge door to themselves under the presumption that 'I thought you knew already.' And here's me just thinking I'm a busy guy.

This attention disorder deficit thing affects my writing - No shit, I hear you say. So sometimes I'll be telling a story and well here we are: Far far away from the first couple of paragraphs. So let's get back on it.

I knew Steve* (Ozzy's PA) from a previous celebrity encounter when he was publicly assisting or maybe even privately assisting - what the fuck does PA even mean, shit acronym, really - Russell Brand. Russell was my first A-lister. Can he still be considered an A-lister ? I find his latest incarnation as spokesperson for the new age warriors sat in his fucking mansion all a little bit tiresome to be honest - but his heart was/is in the right place. And so was his Ashtanga Yoga Primary Series. I taught Russell every day for a week in some posh hotel in Manchester. It was a case of turn up put him through his yoga paces then naff off before he told any jokes. Apparently the news was he'd packed in saluting the H dragon in exchange for saluting the sun a la Ashtanga Yoga. A mate of mine calls Ashtanga a yoga practice for obsessive Westerners, which always makes me smile. Me n our Russ gud ol' fashioned Western obsessives. But after that week I put it at the top of my CV in capital letters RUSSELL BRAND'S YOGA TEACHER. I couldn't give a toss I'd only taught him a few times. He was now my best mate and I was his Yoga GURU and my one to one lessons were now A list expensive. Fuck you Mike Baldwin.

So fast forward maybe 10 or so years. I'd gone from the Manchester streets that were paved with lots and lots of fucking rain to the darling how fabulous streets of Los Angeles. You can read all about that journey in the blog called 'Matt, why are you faking a smile? Have you gone all LA on us? 'It's not a fake smile I'm grimacing ya daft cow I've just had a vasectomy.' True Story.

A number I didn't know blew up on my cell phone (Yes I'm using American vernacular here, well I was in LA -is that ok McLovin** ?)

Steve - Hi Matt it's Steve.

Me (not having a fucking clue who Steve is) - Hi Steve, great to hear from you mate. How's things.

Steve- Things are great, Matt. I'm now working with Ozzy Osbourne. Can you come over to his place in the Hollywood Hills to teach him yoga?

Me- Mark ya daft cunt is that you?

Steve- Pardon

Me (realising it's not me daft mate and trying not to sound like IVE FUCKING ARRIVED whilst running around my apartment punching the air) Ozzy Osbourne? Yes of course - let me get my diary.

Me (puts down phone and starts to open and shut kitchen drawers to sound like I'm looking for my non-existent diary which was full of non-existent A lister celebrity clients.) Ah, got it. Great when does he want to start?

Steve filled me in a few details. Apparently Ozzy had recently done some Goat Yoga. Now if this was for someone off Coronation Street I would have told them to fuck off and put the phone down. But this was Ozzy and for Ozzy I would keep it to myself that I thought Goat Fucking Yoga was fucking stupid and anyone, anyone fucking stupid enough to do it was obviously a dickhead and under no circumstances would I be teaching them yoga. But they were offering me $500 a lesson and for that kind of dough I would have dressed up as a fucking goat.

I was booked in for 2pm a week on Thursday. Finally! Finally I had arrived properly on the streets that have no shame of Los Angeles. Goat Yoga - fabulous darling can you pay me in cash? Steve had told me that under no circumstances was I to mention the Ozzy teaching gig to anyone - not even my priest. In fact the first thing I had to do chez Ozzy was to sign a NDA - a non-disclosure agreement meaning that I was bound by law to keep my trap shut and not tell anyone anything about how good or bad Ozzy's downward dog was. Yeah right mate. As soon as I put the phone down to Steve I had created a new What's App group called Bat Eater Teacher and put EVERY SINGLE FRIEND AND FAMILY MEMBER in the chat.

Wednesday (the day before me n Ozzy were supposed to get bizzy with da yoga):

Steve (via text) - Hi Matt, can we reschedule Ozzy's yoga lesson? He's got an important meeting with Sharon tomorrow now.

Me (via text) - No you fucking can't. Tell Sharon to fuck off and organise the meeting for another day.

Ok so I didn't write that but I wanted to. I texted back something along the lines of: Yes of course that's absolutely fine that means I can go earlier to Tom Cruise's place. I'm teaching him Scientology yoga I have to dress up as a Thetan.

Yes yes ok. I didn't write that either but I will next time. Well, there won't be a next time. Not with the ol' Ozz-man.

I knew from the moment that I got the Ozzy teaching gig that the chances of going more than once were pretty much non-existent. This is how most famous people yoga teaching gigs play out. Famous Person sees other famous person doing yoga and getting good press out of it, so they decide I'll have a bit of that action, I could do with some good press stories. I guess Ozzy couldn't care less about positive or negative news stories but still. So the famous person buys the Gucci Yoga Mat and the Gucci leotard (that's an interesting image: Ozzy in Gucci, darling) they do one fucking lesson then quit and move onto the next potential practice that could get them on the front page of whatever naff celebrity mag everyone's reading. Oh, cynical me! And well this particular famous person teaching gig didn't get past the first hurdle of an actual sodding lesson.

The class was rescheduled for the following Thursday.

The Wednesday before that fucking Thursday:

Steve (via text) - Hi Matt, unfortunately Ozzy has got an ingrowing toe nail - can we reschedule?

Me (via text) - Ok fine

When you text Ok fine it basically means you cunt.

So this same game played out over the next few weeks. The week after that Ozzy is having an operation. The week after he was away on business and yadder yadder yadder. Eventually they just stopped and the game was over. I was gutted. I had my whole Ozzy and Me autobiography already written. My yearlong 'An evening with Ozzy Osbourne's yoga teacher' events were cancelled. I would no longer be dining out on the Ozzy Osbourne's yoga teacher - I couldn't add his name above Russell's on my CV.

What the fuck, I shrugged, finally realising there was a silver lining to this whole shit show. Maybe I can't be the guy that taught Ozzy Yoga but fuck me, surely there's a market for the guy who nearly taught Ozzy yoga - and yes that's you schmuko ;).

* name changed

** if you know , you know.

Who is your practice for?

June 2020

Every so often I'll be listening to a podcast or reading a book and I'll hear/read something that just completely blows me away. Case in point, I was listening to a podcast just last week – podcasts are the new Rock n' Roll for me – any moment I've got two minutes to myself I'm pod-ing up to the max. This particular podcast was a recording of a short talk by über cool Zen dude Henry Shukman of Mountain Cloud Zen gaff – go check out their site now (well after you've finished reading this blog). Henry was talking about the importance of daily Zen practice and almost as a throwaway line he said, 'Who is your practice for?' I didn't catch the full weight of the quote to begin with. In fact, it had bypassed me at first but then my 'Zendar' went up to eleven and I pressed rewind – well not quite, I just pressed that button that allows you to rewind 15 seconds at a time.

'Who is your practice for?' Henry went on as if that statement had no particular value. I stopped the talk and stopped the car (I always like to pod n drive) and sat in the car by the side of the road for a full 15 minutes thinking about who exactly is my practice for. And when I say practice for me that's twofold, as I'm doing this yoga thang and have been doing for over 20 years plus (yikes that's a very long time) and for the past 10 years or so I've been staring at a wall doing the zazen Zen meditation ting. So like anybody who does any type of mind and/or body practice, we are usually doing it for me, myself, and I. I practice yoga as it gives *me* a strong flexible balanced body; I practice meditation because it helps *my* mind. But when you drill down a little on who is your practice for, you suddenly realise, like I did in a light bulb 'ah ha' type moment, that actually I'm not the only who one who benefits from these disciplines.

When I thought about it for some time I actually realised I'm probably the *least* important person on the list of benefiters of these yoga and Zen practices I'm doing. Obviously my wife and kids were the first people on the list – and they benefit in all kinds of ways, a better husband, a fun dad, et cetera. Also I'm a much better person to be around when I've done practice. I was gonna say the 'my' word, as in 'my practice' and that I think is problematic as it sets up in your own mind that the practice is all about lil 'ol me – well it's not – get over it! I've been in Mysore, in the south of India a whole bunch of times and the practice narcissism is off the scale. Nearly everyone is talking about 'my practice.' 'Oh my practice was great,' 'my practice was terrible,' and then 'that's enough about my practice what do you think about my practice'...

So talking of narcissism, back to me 😊. Post practice(s) I can think more clearly and I don't put my foot in my mouth (or around my head, yoga joke - eyes rolling emoji) as much as I do normally. And that good vibz ripple effect goes out into the universe in a *it's nice to be nice, smile at someone and make their day* stylee. Obviously not everyone is gonna pass it along, and that doesn't matter. The fact that you started the post practice wave is all that counts.

Practicing pretty much continuously for over 20 years has 100% made me a better teacher (see below to judge for yourself) and a more compassionate, less selfish person. (I still completely lose my s,h,one t when I'm watching the football though, Rome wasn't built in a day or even in 20 + years!) Just thinking about it, if I add the folk I'm teaching yoga to every evening and add in their circle of friends and family, dogs, cats, and fish, you soon get the picture.

And I'm not one of those folk who get on the 'my way or the highway yoga bandwagon.' Yoga (and zazen) just happen to be the things that work for me – and when I say work for me, one of my teaching philosophies ,if you can call it that, is I think as human folk we all have a responsibility to ourselves and to each other to find the right combo of mind/body practices that help us be a lil better to ourselves and those around us – and in turn those around us be a lil better to those around them. So whether you are a yogi or a mediator or a knitter or a crown green bowler it disnae matter. Make your choices and join in the *make yoself a better person* fun.

And whilst you're at that make a mental list of all the potential people (and dogs n cats too if you like) who will benefit from those practices besides yourself.

I got 99 Problems, but Ashtanga ain't one !

May 2018

Ashtanga Yoga is experiencing some fairly intense turbulence at the moment – I don't want to get into a discussion about reasons as to why in this blog – I don't think I'm either qualified or well informed enough to make any valid comment. At the moment I'm guessing I'm similar to quite a few Ashtanga teachers in that we are still trying to process and make sense of information we are coming into contact with- holding the tension between this 'information' and the love & respect we have in our hearts for the practice and its teachers.From a personal perspective I can tell you it's a real head fuck (apologies for the f bomb there but in the circumstances I felt it necessary).

What is interesting to read recently is folk's opinions on the actual practice of Ashtanga Yoga (well I say opinion but most of what I'm reading is judgement very thinly disguised as opinion),and some of these folks have never been to Mysore or even practiced Ashtanga with any regularity to have anything relevant to say.

A few things that I would like to comment on are:

1.Ashtanga Yoga is a heavily Asana based discipline and personally I'm very happy with that.When I've done the practice I feel good physically and mentally , and I'm a much, much better person to people I come into contact with post practice (including myself). I'm happy with its structure in the way that it's taught and that postures are added to ones practice once competence and understanding is achieved in the postures previous to the ones that are subsequently added. I'm pretty sure some people don't like this system – I'm also pretty sure that usually most if not all of these people go off and find a different yoga system thats better suited to them.For me it's a little like the cliche of digging a hole for water , if you don't dig deep enough you'll just end up with lots of shallow holes and no water.I've been practicing 20 years now and the (Ashtanga) water tastes sweet ! As a caveat to this I'm pretty sure that the peace and sense of well-being that one gets from Ashtanga is the same for whatever level of physical practice you are at ie you don't need to be able to stick yer legs behind your head to feel super dooper post practice. Also it's absolute none sense to think that a postural hierarchy (the more postures you can do the more ace you are) exists for all Ashtangis -as someone who has been immersed in the practice for 20 years (ie C'est Moi) I can tell you categorically it's a very tiny group of folk who get caught up in the ' I can do this posture , ain't I just fabulous' mentality.

2 I don't need to read the Yoga Sutras /BhagavadGita to tell me how to live my life – but I know students who swear by both books I'm just not one of them and that's OK-we're all different after all. I have this thing that I think every human being on the planet has a responsibility to themselves to find the right set of practices that suit them – that are able to guide them to lead a more fulfilling life. I've found the practice of Ashtanga and Zen meditation to be the winning combo for me ! The appropriate phrase above being 'responsibility to themselves' ie take some responsibility for yourself in how you live your life. In the Zen tradition if you try and give the teacher / master your responsibility (the responsibility that says please tell me how to live my life) s/he'll tell you to piss off (in a Zen way of course). My very own Zen teacher Brad Warner has told me to piss off loads of times – not in a I don't care about you type way, but in a manner which made me think through things a little more , accept myself and who I am – warts and all. To quote Brad quoting Bill & Ted 'I can't tell you how to live your life other than be excellent to each other'

3 No one on the planet has the ability to see into the heart and mind of another person – we are unable to know just what another person feels. Just because one person doesn't fall in line with what you think they should do/say doesn't make them wrong and you right.Have a think about that before you start throwing your judgements around.

4 I've had some terrible experiences when I've been in Mysore (including a 3 day toilet 'meditation' intensive-also having to wait over 2 hours to get on the mat at the old shala every day for 2 months wasn't that fabulous either.One time I had to sit on those bloody stairs in the old shala and listen to a couple of students prattle on about their chakras needing a resetting – I'm from Manchester we don't do chakras our kid!). I've also had some quite extraordinary amazing experiences there – I got married Hindu Style (see video below) on Chamundi Hill which was very magical. Practicing Ashtanga in the very place it comes from felt special too. On reflection the place holds some very magical memories for me that's for sure.

5 I love social media / I hate social media – no that isn't a Zen koan but the push pull in my mind about Facebook twitter Instagram etc etc. As much damage as these online platforms can create I do think they are of some use. They can and do act as a mega phone for plenty of mega idiots sounding off as if the whole digital world need to hear what they've got to say -but I think they could help draw folks attention to (yoga)things that need drawing attention to! For example I'm an Ashtanga teacher a large percentage of what I teach is called Mysore Style (Google if you have no idea what this is , I'm trying to keep my blogs under a 5 minute read and we are up to 4.38 at this point so I'll need to finish up soon and if I start blathering on about what Mysore style is, the blog will be nearer a 7 minute read and the stats show that's just way too long for people to concentrate on mediocre writing

by a 2nd rate Ashtanga teacher). Anyway so if I give a bad adjustment and continue doing so to different students well it'll only be a matter of time before I'm outed on the inter webs as incompetent – that I'm a crap teacher will be shared around the yogaweb and then it'll only be a matter of time before I'll have to hang up shorts and look for a new career. With that in mind that's gonna keep me on my yoga toes to make sure I'm keeping it real in the shala – I'm sure in time there will be a yelp star system for quality of adjustments in Ashtanga studios .Hey Ashtanga naysayers whilst you're trying to dismantle the house of Ashtanga for your own advancement maybe add that to your list of things to do- good luck 😌.

Yoga Mind Beginners Mind

December 2022

So first things first yes I nicked the title from the famous book 'Zen Mind Beginners Mind' by Zen master Shunryu Suzuki – all will be revealed why in the content of this blog.

Right I have no idea why I am writing a blog , nobody reads these days so I promise to keep it short.

I was actually thinking about donning a tiny pair of speedos and throwing a few yoga shapes whilst showing a bit of ass on an Instagram reel in the hope of getting strangers to like me but well I thought I'd write something instead. I don't want to do that whole social media rant thing here as I'm trying to write something purposeful that maybe people might connect with and either agree or disagree, but it's very tempting.

FUCK YOU social media – right, got that out of my system. Shall we begin ?

In the Zen book mentioned above there's a line (well there's a few, that's why it's a book and not a social fucking media spiritual meme -arghh I'm at it again , let it go Ryan let it go).

The line goes something like this ..

'In a beginners mind there are many possibilities, in an experts mind there are few'.

So my layman's interpretation is that one should maintain a fresh open perspective in life and in practice – which we could say are macrocosm / microcosm, and not think that we know it all.

Getting back into teaching real people recently (and finally moving away from teaching tiny people in a box on a laptop) I stumbled into this line trying to explain to folk that every time you get on the mat , it's a fresh new experience. Your body and mind are different to how they both were last time you practiced. But there's always a temptation to slip into the expert mind of ' I need to bind in Marichyasana A or catch ankles in Kapotasana delete as appropriate. But you get my drift. Our whole practice takes on a life of is it as good / bad as the last time we practiced, the judging mind shit that moves us away from our fresh new experience of a beginners mind. Yes I get it – we are westerners, we have that 'we must achieve at all costs' written into our DNA. But Yoga is not a destination as the cliché goes but a journey. Put it another way and to quote Henry Miller in his ace book Big Sur and the Oranges of Hieronymus Bosch..

'A person's destination is never a place but rather a new way of looking at things'.

Read that line again as it blew me away when I read the book. A person's destination is never a place but rather a new way of looking at things. Boom. Can you apply that philosophy when you're next on the mat ? Don't look at practice as Surya Namaskar being the starting line with 'taking rest' the finishing, but as an opportunity to have a fresh new experience.

I was just yesterday listening to a podcast with the total Zentastic Dude Rick Rubin (Broken Record podcast – absolutely ace – go check it out.). He was chatting with top Hip Hoppers Run the Jewels (and if you aint heard these boy's bars , stop right now and go listen I implore you!) El-P was talking about some lyrics that he had written but he wasn't happy with a couple of bars, so the whole song didn't feel right. Eventually he was able to write something new and this changed the whole expression/ feeling of the song that he was totally happy with. I think there's also something to be learned from that attitude. And it's something that I totally resonate with. Sometimes practice doesn't feel right , perhaps it's a certain posture that I have done a certain way over a period of time but it has become a little uncomfortable and eventually I have the insight to move things round a little, and everything clicks again.

Some years ago I was talking with a student about the Ashtanga Yoga system. She was bored with Primary Series – 'if I have to do Janu A again I'll scream' she said. It would have been quite easy here to do that thing that Ashtangis like to do and get on the Ashtanga soapbox to preach the gospel of Patanjali. Ok so most of you know I don't jive to the Yoga Sutra ting but sure there's something in there about continued practice and blah blah blah – in fact note to self-re-write the Sutras as the Yoga Blah of Patanjali*. So I told her to go off and explore other yoga systems and find something that she resonates with. I mentioned (to her) that for me the most important thing to look for is the lineage and tradition of the system – she agreed and went off a joined a hot yoga studio.**

Back to the point of this blog. After the above chat with me student I went away and thought just what is it that keeps me returning daily to Ashtanga and to Janu A – (hey Janu A big up yoself). And to nick another book title from Mr.(O)G 'My experiments with the truth' I feel every time I get on the mat it's an experiment with Ashtanga Yoga. What is happening to my body and mind during each posture and each vinyasa – every time is different, something new to explore both in mind and body. It never ever gets boring – quite the opposite – there's always something new – every day. It really is maintaining that beginners mind. And I try to embrace beginners mind when I'm teaching too – everyone's mind and body is different -and different every day – as me main Verve man Dicky Ashcroft sang 'we're a million different people from one day to the next'. Teaching – especially Mysore Style, I feel it's as important for the student as it is for me to maintain beginners mind.

I guess here would be as good as any place to address my thoughts on the Ashtanga Yoga system and its tradition. From the outside looking in (and sometimes from the inside looking in too) it's easy to see these various sequences as a linear tiered system to develop and achieve. Primary Series, Second Series Third Fourth etc 'Hey Man check me I'm doing third series I have arrived baby' is the Instagram post inference usually with a quote from that man again Patanjali. I love how these folk post pictures of themselves yoga pretzeled to the max and then use some naff spiritual cliché to make you believe just how awake they are – I mean what's wrong with telling us how awake you are in Janu A ? Sorry went off piste a little there. So I think it's good to look at the Ashtanga sequences in reverse order – so Primary Series comes in first place. In fact Pattabhi Jois said somewhere that 'Primary Series is most important, Second Series is of some importance and the advanced series is for insta reels only (ok he actually said advanced series for demonstration only, but I just updated it).

The word tradition gets banded about too. The tradition is this, the tradition is that and blah fucking blah. Can we use a different word instead of tradition? And I'm going to put forward the word 'trend'! As that what I see – the Ashtanga Yoga system has evolved for better or worse and we know P.J. taught differently to different students – which how it should be. Individualise the system for the individual – makes sense no? For some students Bhujapidasana is not and might never be appropriate but Baddha Konasana and Upavishta Konasana are. But hey wait the tradition says unless the student is binding in Marichyasana D they can no longer continue with the rest of the primary series. Er well that idea of the tradition makes absolutely NO SENSE (maybe I can add an N between the O and the S). Maybe let's see if we can add in a dose of beginners mind here – up north we have a different phrase for beginners mind – common fucking sense (add in the word fucking as appropriate – I love a good F bomb as you can tell by my total lack of sophistication in my writing – but please feel free to leave it out). My aim is to (and apologies to readers who have an aversion to anything that could be construed as 'woo woo') to turn the student into the Guru – and definitely not pretend to be one myself. And when I say turn the student into a Guru what I mean by this that I try to get them to understand their own bodies and it's limitations and the posture(s) they are doing and fit them two things together that allows them to maintain a steady breath , steady body and steady gaze. Easy init.

** Did you ever see the Charlie Brown cartoon? You know when the school Principle gets on the tannoy system and the voice comes out as mwah mwah mwah mwah – ie not real words but just muffled sounds ?Well this is what my brain does to the Patanjali Sutras when I try to read them.

* ok ok this is a joke and hot yoga fans you know I love you really and hot yoga too – it's just so, hot!

Mysore (Ass) Part 2

Sign Up Day, January 2, 2001, Sunday Afternoon, 2ish, Old Shala, Laxmipuram, Mysore

When I made the decision to go to Mysore some months previously I had no idea what I was letting myself in for. I had no idea how popular Ashtanga Yoga was, I did think that maybe there'd be me and another couple of weirdos and that would be it. Well I was right about one thing - weirdos - except there were more than two - there were hundreds of them. All loitering with the intent of signing up to practice with the Ashtanga Yoga guru - Mr. Pattabhi Jois - or Guruji, as he affectionately became known - well for a while. In 2018 - nine years after he'd passed away, he got Me Too'd big time, and the arse fell out of favour in the Ashtanga Yoga lineage. He went from being my late Guruji to the late Pattabhis Jois to that dirty ol' bugger in the blink of a drishti (Ashtanga in joke).

Anyway, here I was like a complete fish out of water standing in line to pay my shala fees wearing my best manc twinset of tee-shirt and jeans. And here was my first yoga fashion faux pas - every other weirdo stood in line all dressed head to toe in what can only be described as bed sheets. Well that's what it looked like to me. Combinations of colours and baggy-ness - I mean I do do baggy but only in jeans not bedsheets, sorry. There was one couple who shall remain nameless stood all dressed in black like Mr and Mrs Count Fucking Dracula - very weird vibes. I believe they left the Ashtanga Yoga community some years later to set up their own system of yoga 'inspired' by the Ashtanga practice - and by 'inspired' I mean they totally ripped it off and added their own nonsense chants and postures names. They even had a vegan cat for fucks sake.

There was a bit of bantz going down in the yoga queue - well when I say bantz folk were arguing over the real meaning of yoga. Yoga is love, said one person. Yoga is the journey to the self, said another. Deary fucking me was my contribution to the discussion. Then all of a sudden the noise quietened down when a black four by four Range Rover type car drove up and parked next to the OG Shala. I thought it might have been Princess Anne but the windows were tinted so I didn't have a clue who it was. Hopefully a Priest with a cross and some garlic to see off The Draculas. Then came the whirring sound of an electric window going down *wwwhhizzzzzz*. A face appeared and it was the Guru, complete with black sunglasses and a tonne of gold bling around his neck. If MC's did yoga... There was an audible gasp from the crowd and someone started to cry. No joke. This is gonna be a long two months, I thought to myself.

Finally after what felt like forever standing in line like I was in some sadomasochistic *how long can you stand in direct sunlight* challenge for a game show, I was ushered in and upstairs to pay my respects and more importantly to pay my dollar to the (ex) Guru! Now I'm gonna be completely honest with you here. I had done some research - not much, but

I'd spent an hour or so surfing the world wide web sussing out what to say and what not what to say, to the Guru. One thing that kept cropping up was the touching or kissing of the feet of the aforementioned wise one. Now this to me was very, very weird but when the going gets tough, the tough gets weird and as I approached the ol fella who was sat next to his money counting machine (I kid you not, the whole place was held together with duct tape and looked like it hadn't been cleaned for a few decades but this crazy ol fool had this state of the art machine that counted notes) I knelt down and kissed the Guru's feet - actually kissed as in puckered my lips and kissed his feet. First right foot, then left foot. I looked up at him and he looked down at me puzzled in a *what the fuck are you doing you stupid western muppet* kind of way. I thought I saw a halo hovering just above his head but I think I was going down with sunstroke. Neither of us moved for ages. Eventually the lord spoketh the holy words of 'You got money?' And I stood up and handed him a big wedge of rupees. I wanted to ask him if we could just forget about that foot thing but thought better of it. I paid my money and got the hell out of there as fast as possible. Fuck out my way Drac, I said under my breath as I pushed past the dark one who was still loitering even though he'd already paid his money. How are you still alive anyway in this sunlight?

Practice Day 1, address as above, about 6am

My first day at the shala very nearly became a non-event, ie I nearly fucked off when I arrived. You see the ol' shala might look good on the Ashtanga Yoga teacher's CV but the reality was it was a big shit show. The OG shala was only big enough for 12 people at a time and when there was over 200 who had signed up to practice - well you do the math. I got there at my allotted time of 6am expecting to go straight in and Ashtanga boogie only to be faced with a big time queue of people sat on the stairs all looking miserable. Hmm. I walked up the stairs and eventually found the end of the line in the small 'take rest' room which was directly above the actual practice room (shala) below. It was here that I first tasted the nectar of the Ashtanga Yoga good vibz for all. In this take rest room, students who had already practiced downstairs came up to lay down and as the title of the room suggests, to take rest. These students had gotten to practice earlier and the word was that the earlier the time slot you were given by the Guru the higher up the Ashtanga food chain you got. So the students who got the 4.30 am time slot were the fully enlightened paid up members of the Ashtanga Yoga version of the Freemasons. They also practiced alone as PJ didn't get out of bed til 5.30 am.

So here I am, sat like an Ashtanga minion at the end of a 'it's gonna be at least 2 hours before you get in that practice room baby' queue. All the other minions were sat perfectly still bolt upright hoping that the Guru might spot their perfect yogic poise, most were reading either The Bhagavad-Gita or The Yoga Sutras of Patanjali - the bibles of Ashtanga. I sat reading my own bible - The autobiography of Bez from the Happy Mondays. As you might have guessed I'm not very good at 'playing the game'. I was just being myself. It felt like I was sat with a load of frauds playing a game, pretending to be more spiritual, or more something - full of shit maybe. Dunno. I don't want to be negative as you know I had a great fucking time in Mysore, eventually. Slowly, very slowly we went down the stairs. One by one you come, came the Guru's instructions from downstairs instructing the next student into the shala. And one by one we moved from one stair to the next.

Practice Day 2, address as above, time as above, The Stairs Incident Part 1

So every day pretty much for the whole two months I was in Mysore I had to wait at least two hours before I could be goin like a boin on the mat- I say at least as some days it was nearly two. On Practice Day 2 I was at the bottom of the stairs which meant I was next in line to go 'take practice'. ONE MORE! PJ would shout and the person sat on the last stair would step onto the hallowed turf of the OG shala. But just as I was sat on the last step, this lass appeared out of nowhere - ready to go in before me. As the ONE MORE instruction came this bloody lass started to make a move on MY spot – 'scuse me mate. I got up double quick and pushed past her and into the shala. She looked a bit startled. But rules are rules init - I had to wait, so should she. After all we are all love and peace and equal. But as I learnt, rules aren't necessarily the same rules for everyone. Especially in the OG Shala. As it turned out, some students are more equal than others. So the gig was if you were an old time student of PJ then you got to forgo the stair marathon and go straight into the shala when a space became available. I didn't like this rule, so I ignored it. I remember a day or two later I was sat in some cafe - ok so this was no Starbucks more like a shack with a couple of tables, when I heard a pair of yoga students speaking loudly with the intent for me to hear them. There's that rude guy who jumped into the Shala before Radha. RESULT: I had only been in the place a couple of days and I had gotten a reputation as a 'rude guy'. You know looking back, as mentioned above, I didn't know the rules or the shala etiquette, it wasn't that I was being intentionally rude, I just don't like and have never liked bullshit.

Practice Day 3, address and time as above, The Stair Incident Part 2

So I spent most of my time at the OG shala sat on those stairs reading Bez's autobiography. I was reading about a different kind of enlightenment - one that was chemically induced.

When one fellow stair minion had the temerity to whisper something to another they got shouted at by one of the aforementioned early morning practice Enlightened crew who was taking rest - BE QUIET CANT YOU SEE WE ARE RESTING - yikes - see that Ashtanga Yoga aint working so good for you pal. Yoga is love eh ? Or is it Yoga is love as long as you keep your gob shut whilst I'm resting after my oh so important yoga practice. My practice is the Mysore student's mantra, oh my practice this my practice that and yadder yadder yadder.

You know, or maybe you don't know that all of the stories in this book are 100% true - granted I might add a soupçon of manc-ness here and there plus some floral language in the shape of an f bomb or three. But it's all true.

Practice Day 4, address as above time as above, The Money Incident Part 1

So Shala fees went something like this. One month was 3000 rupees and for every month after that the fees went down to 2000 rupees. I only found out about this pricing structure after I'd already given PJ 6000 rupees. I'll give the ol man the benefit of the doubt, as he was probably still shell shocked at this freak actually kissing his feet, he didn't notice that I'd given him 6000 instead of 5000 rupees for my two months shala fees. So on Day 4 after I'd found out about the 2nd month discount I approached the Guru. Er hello Gerugee - so ok yes I was drinking the Kool Aid a little by addressing him as Guruji but ya know I'd already caused a fuss with the refusal to play the Ashtanga hierarchy stair game, I didn't want to run the risk of being run out of town by the Shala Police. (The Shala Police are the self-appointed holier than thou Ashtanga students who have taken it upon themselves to make sure everyone falls in line - they are a rather joyless lot - I suspect they've probably never taken ecstasy).

Me -I think I gave you too much money for my shala fees.

PJ - checking checking checking

And that was all he said.

Practice Day 5, address as above time as above, The Money Incident Part 2

As I walked into the shala I was just about to climb the stairs when PJ appeared out of nowhere like a Yoga version of Mr. Ben and handed me a $100 note. That was it. A refund. A result.

One thing that I did take to Mysore was a Parka. Well I am from Manchester and thought it would be rude not to. So when I say Parka I don't mean one of those big sleeping bag things that Liam wears, it was more of a wind breaker type vibe. As the temperature in Mysore was HOTTER THAN THE SUN most days the brand new parka stayed in the backpack. Finally the sun disappeared one day, the temperature dropped, and it was parka time. It was blue, it had a hood, and I looked pretty fucking cool in it if I'm being honest. I was stood with a couple of yoga students I vaguely knew when I pulled out the aforementioned and proudly zipped the bugger up (right up to the chin as that's the proper manc way init). As I was zipping up, I noticed the cardboard price tag was still attached to the zipper, so calm as cool as you like without anyone noticing I removed it and folded it up a few times and kept in my hand. Now sometimes I do things on purpose and other times (well most times) I do things off the cuff (without engaging my brain). I surreptitiously handed the folded up piece of cardboard to one of these yoga students' types and bizarrely enough this person took it without asking what it was. One of the other yoga student types noticed and enquired..

What's that you've just handed over

Me – Keep it quiet but it's a gram of Charlie *

Yoga Type*** – oh wow , I would love a bit of Charles **

Now at this point I just walked off without letting the Yoga Type know I was just pulling her leg. I was actually shaking with laughter that 1) this person thought I actually had some cocaine and was giving it to someone else and 2) in this Land of Yoga (some) people were up for a bit of the Columbian Marching Powder. Now I'm not saying that every Tom Dick and Anand yoga student in Mysore would wanna bit of nose bag action and maybe this person was a one off, but ya know to me it just fed into the large amount of BS I smelt at times around certain people and their own sense of holier than thou spiritual self-importance.

* Charlie is one of the many 'street' names for Cocaine

** Charles is definitely NOT one of the street names for Cocaine, but a phrase used by idiots who have probably never taken the stuff. Not that I'm saying it's good to take cocaine – in fact kids stay away from it – it is the devil's work.

*** Not mentioning any names here but this Yoga Type person was one of the 'movers' and 'shakers' of the aforementioned Ashtanga Police.

In 2005 The Mountain came to Muhammed as The Pattabhi Jois roadshow came to (London) town and yours truly booked himself a place to attend the week long Second Series led Class that PJ was teaching. On the first day I rocked up to see a front row of the Ashtanga Yogarati – the top dogs from the Ashtanga World. Right, fuck this, I thought and muscled myself in between a couple of the top dogs. I'll be on the front row too, thank you very much! After a week of busting my second series ass I stood in line to fist bump the Guru (and not kiss the poor buggers feet!). When I got myself to the front of the queue PJ looked at me, smiled, and said 'You come to Mysore!' which kinda burst my good vibz bubble as I said back to him 'Ive already been... twice!' He just laughed. A yoga friend comforted me and said that the fact that PJ had asked me to go to Mysore was a good sign, he doesn't say that to everyone.

Ashtanga You Do, Ashtanga You Don't

May 2016

If you ever strike it lucky and manage to get yourself booked into the shala in Mysore, South India – which to be honest is becoming harder and harder these days, it's a real lottery if you get accepted or not (in fact it's probably easier to win the bloody lottery) - you will have to adhere to the Shala's codes of practice. Which if you don't know, go something like this...

Everyone, and I mean everyone (including yoga celebs like Kino MacGregor and Eddie Stern), has to practice primary series on their first week (minimum booking 1 month, maximum 3 months) regardless of what series they are on. First week primary only, it's the law, no discussions, nuff said. After that first week you are then allowed to practice whatever series you were doing last time you were at the shala and if you've never been before you stay in primary series until Sharath deems your practice good enough to move you into intermediate series. So when I say good enough what I actually mean is that you have a good understanding both physically and mentally of all the postures in the sequence. If you're relatively new to Ashtanga the rule (in the shala) is until you are able to 'bind' (ie, clasp the hands behind your back) in Marichyasana D then you do the next posture which is navasana then move straight into the closing sequence of asanas without even attempting the post navasana postures.

Some people are ok with this. Some people get a little hot under the collar about it. Especially as the (very good) argument for folk getting antsy about that rule is that there are postures beyond navasana in the sequence that are very good for beginners (baddha konasana, upavistha konasana, etc) and when I say good I mean good as in appropriate or suitable.

Speaking to all the old school Ashtanga Yoga students like David Swenson, they say that Guruji Pattabhi Jois would never really stop a student from practicing the whole sequence – only in certain circumstances. I guess the main reason for allowing students to continue to practice the whole series was down to the fact that there wasn't that many students attending the shala in the old days so Guruji would be able to keep his eye on everyone to make sure they weren't doing anything untoward and injuring themselves. But over the years the Shala got double busy and in 2002 a brand new shiny shala opened that could accommodate up to 80 students at a time – the old shala was only big enough for 12. So now it was much harder for both Guruji and Sharath to be able to keep their eyes on 80 students and the above rule of being able to bind in Marichyasana D was enforced. I guess mainly to stop the newer or less experienced students from throwing themselves around the mat and hurting themselves. Makes sense to me. Also another very good reason for this rule (which also applies once you start doing other sequences, like if you can't get your leg behind your head in eka pada sirsasana in the intermediate series that's where you would be stopped until you are able to do this posture safely and comfortably) is that it helps to keep the 'check my practice out' ego maniacs in check – which I've witnessed plenty of times in Mysore.

Unfortunately this bind rule has been applied I think too literally in the past for the wrong circumstances and wrong reasons and I for one have been very guilty of that. I remember a few years back it was just after I got my fabulous Level 2 authorisation from the Shala and I was teaching a Mysore class in Manchester. One of my regulars who used to come to every class I taught was moving her way slowly and steadily through the practice. Now this lady wasn't able to bind in Marichyasana D but usually as there were only around 10 or so folk at class I was able to help her and others navigate through the more difficult postures beyond navasana. But now I had the authorisation so I must apply the Shala rules. I explained to the student just why I wasn't allowing her to continue beyond navasana and asked her to start the finishing sequence which she did, albeit with tears in her eyes. She thought she had done something wrong. She hadn't, but I had – big time. That was the first and last occasion that I ever stopped someone in inappropriate circumstances. (I later apologised to the student so all good!)

A few years after the above incident I was teaching someone privately at my house in Manchester. The student was going to a different Ashtanga teacher in a different area – and despite this student practicing for nearly two years they were being asked to stop at navasana by their other teacher. This person was able to bind in marichyasana D (albeit on one side only) but as they started to go through their practice with me I could tell that the student had a good understanding of the practice, their body, and their body's limitations. It was a one to one situation and I felt quite comfortable taking them through the whole sequence – especially as the baddha konasana posture was going to be very good for their stiff hips. I was able to break down section by section the three more difficult postures post navasana in a way that they now had a good understanding of these postures and how to do them on their own in a safe way. After all, let us not kid ourselves, it's not rocket science here, is it? The student loved the class so much so they booked me again the next day.

A few days later after the student had gone back 'darn sarf' (or was it up north, I can't quite remember) I got a text message from him saying that his other teacher wasn't very happy about me taking him through the whole practice. I had explained during the class why I thought it was appropriate to take him through the whole thing and also the reasons why his other teacher might be stopping him (busy shala perhaps), and also as it's a one to one it's a safe environment - so all good in my eyes. He also mentioned that the teacher had suggested that he (should) change certain aspects about the way he was living his life which kinda took me by surprise. I told my young Padawan (well by text, longest text message I ever sent – it was bloody *War & Peace* on a mobile phone) that in my opinion the only legitimate person who should be telling someone how to live their life was themselves – and that they shouldn't in no uncertain circumstances be handing that particular authority to anyone else. He should accept and take responsibility for his own life. Yes it's good to take advice from yoga teachers but when they are telling you need to change certain aspects of your life that you enjoy (and not in any way detrimental to your health) then you have to just let go of that advice. And ultimately give it up for what? Just so he can bind on both sides in marichyasana D .. go figure.

Buddhist teacher and academic Stephen Batchelor explains that the practice of meditation is not an end in itself but a practice so one can live a more fulfilling life – whether it's enjoying a piece of art, a walk in the park, or maybe the opera, whatever. For me, Yoga serves exactly the same purpose. Yes, there are physical benefits of a stronger, more flexible body, etc. but my Yoga practice allows me to enjoy more the time I spend with my family or even a fine green tea. And anyone with a modicum of intelligence will tell you that the ability to bind in marichyasana D has no bearing WHATSOEVER on how a yoga practice can positively impact your life.

In the words of David Swenson...

'Don't let yoga ruin your life'

ie, don't get too caught up in what postures you can and can't do – and certainly don't stop enjoying life in its entirety. Allowing your life to be about one thing only can be very destabilising emotionally, physically, even spirituality (if you're that way inclined).

,ding to fix the Break (the drugs do work)

December 2022

First up a massive, massive shout out to everyone who reached out to me either on social media or personally after I posted my last blog. As I mentioned in it, I think it can be kind of tragic when people play out their personal lives on social media and only wrote if after I was persuaded by a friend. Any road, thank you for your warmth, affection, and love. It really did bring more than a few tears to my eyes.

So don't worry this is not a Part 2. Well, not in a direct way. It's more of an addendum to that aforementioned blog. Despite the love, managing depersonalisation disorder and an impending divorce ain't as fun as it sounds. A very good friend of mine from God's own land (and also a GP) suggested I take another look at western medicine. Now I haven't taken medication for DPD for a good few years mainly because it doesn't actually fucking work, or certainly hasn't worked. There's medication for the depression and anxiety that DPD causes but nowt' for the DPD itself. But my friends are persuasive buggers. I relented and got (western) med'd up to the max and yikes, some breathing space actually came my way.

I'm telling you all this rather personal stuff not for more love (although happy to accept whatever you got) but to put it out there that even the folk that work to fix other people get broken sometimes. Yoga is such an incredible tool for the mind and body, but it would be foolhardy to suggest it's a magic wand. It isn't. But it can help. There's a rather cute yoga Instagram meme doing the rounds with a heading 'I bend so I don't break,' the obvious inference being that if we practice Yoga then this will keep the mind wolves at bay. But what happens when we do break? As the chances of breaking are like very, very high and pretty inevitable. What was it the Buddha said? 'Life is suffering' or more bluntly: In your life at some point shit happens and you are gonna suffer, directly and indirectly. What happens then – has yoga forsaken us ? Course not, the yoga show must go on and we can rephrase the meme to bending to fix the break which is a more plausible statement. So shout out to all yoga teachers on da 'gram: Can we please, please stop with the 'Yoga makes me bullet proof and aint life just peachy, darling?' rhetoric. Lets get on the honesty vibe of #bendingtofixthebreak posts. Thank you. As you were, or are, or well, carry on reading....

As I sat with my therapist the other day (yep, this yogi is well and truly broken, I'm back on the medicine again, and having regular talk therapy) I gave him the cliche of first world problems as opposed to third world problems. Mate I've been to India so I know just how tough life can be. But he came back with: Third world/first world, they are still problems and problems in whichever world are problems. And we need to use whatever means necessary to figure our shit out.

My guy also told me about the practice of Japanese Kintsugi -golden joinery or golden repair. It is the Japanese art of repairing broken pottery by mending the areas of breakage with lacquer dusted or mixed with powdered gold, silver, or platinum. So it's essentially about finding beauty, character and meaning in the broken – how incredibly beautiful is that?

I was listening to a podcast recently with one of my absolute heroes Rick Rubin. Now Rick had starting meditating when he was 14 (apparently he had hurt his neck and a doctor had recommended he try meditating to help with the pain). He's known in the music industry as an uber-hip Zen legend. But in his early 30's he'd went into a very deep depression that he had no idea how to get out of. His long term meditation practice didn't help any. Eventually Rick was persuaded to take meds and after a little bit of trial and error finding the right one things started to ease up. He quite publicly puts that easing up down to pharmacology. Interestingly enough on his own podcast 'Broken Record' there's an ace episode of Rick interviewing Bruce Springsteen. And The Boss tells of a similar story to Rick's when in his early thirties he too had gone into a darkness that was resolved due to finding the right meds.

So here we've got two incredible people and might we say geniuses – leaders in their field with the world at their feet both going into a deep depression and were able to use meds to fix their break. Ok so please note that NOT for one hot minute am I advocating anyone who suffers with any kind of mental health problem be quick to jump on the medication bandwagon coz I aint. But I think the right idea is to be open to anything and everything that could help. Yoga, meditation, medication, you dig? I guess there's this idea that as a Zen practicing Yoga teacher for 25 years or so I should be able to use asana and meditation instead of medication but why not use both if the cap fits, eh?

The room where I sleep, in the house that I part own, feels like a physical manifestation of my life and my mind. It's easy to get lost in ones own pity party shit show. The night before my writing this, I try to fall asleep in this room of doom of mine. My mind runs away with itself as I think about a couple of lines in a song I wrote years ago,

Looking back across my life

I can't see too much that I like

The small room contains a couple of boxes of clothes, a guitar, and a few bags of books. I sigh and think: Fucking hell, here at the age of 53 is the sum total of my life before my very own eyes. What a fucking failure I am! But within minutes of entering the pity party, I'm watching a documentary of the actor Jonah Hill talking with his therapist (on Netflix called Stutz – well worth a watch). His therapist has practical actions and strategies one can take to improve their lives. He talks about one being a metaphor of a string of pearls, where one can look practically at positive aspects of their lives. Even the simple act of waking up and breathing can be a pearl on the string. I sit and think about where my own pearls can be found. I don't need to look far as I've got two snuggled up either side of me fast asleep in the shape of a pair of my kids. Easy and Boo are just incredible children and people – much like their older siblings. So, there, boom! Four pearls on my string before I've even had breakfast.

In the morning after the night before I'm catching a train to Edinburgh where I've been invited to teach Mysore Style traditional Ashtanga Yoga. Yes, invited by someone I don't know who found me on t'intent and thought enough about me that they want me to go to their studio in Edinburgh and teach their students – and pay me for the trouble. At least three pearls there to go on the string. And well before I know it I got a couple of pearl necklaces worth of good vibz. Sometimes you don't have to look too far to find your own pearl, sometimes it's right under your nose (the fact you are breathing surely has to be a pretty good shout for a pearl, no?).

I'm on the train to Edinburgh finishing this blog off. Another guest of Rick Rubin's Broken Record podcast is Questlove – top drummer from The Roots and all round decent bloke. Questlove has another strategy to stay positive. Every day before he actually gets out of bed he mentally lists 20 positive affirmations – and similar to the string of pearls above these can be anything from I'm awake and I'm alive and breathing to I've got ace kids/ partner/dog/cat/yoga zen... you get the drift.

We are all in the gutter, but some of us are looking at the stars, said Quentin Crisp, and boy oh boy is it easy to stay festering in the gutter and ignore the stars. But the stars are there for EVERYONE all we need to do is look for them.

Happy BIG Shining Stars to you all – stay beautiful and be excellent to each other, go tell someone you love them.

Depersonalisation – The Drugs don't work , but the Ashtanga does

October 2022

Ok I'll let you know from the get go that this is gonna be a bit of a struggle for us both. It's not going to make for easy reading, but my good friend Chandler has challenged me to write something as it might prove be therapeutic – in a get it all out there kind of way. I'm a little apprehensive about letting the world in to my very personal struggle with a very little known mental disorder called Depersonalisation – depersona-what you might say? And yep, don't worry if you've never heard of it, as it turns out there's plenty of medical folk who don't know what it is either.

So we need to go back, way back to my late teens, maybe 17 or 18. I was living with my Mum and her second husband in the rather fabulous (not) town of Baguley in Manchester. I used to do this strange thing of looking at myself in a mirror. After maybe a few moments I would enter into an alternate state which, to be honest, would scare the shit out of me. As soon as I got myself into those states I would then have to go and put some music on or play the guitar to get myself together again, to get back into me. During these alternate states I would disappear. I would no longer be a self – yes I know this sounds batshit crazy but it's the only way I can articulate it. There might be a handful of people reading this who will have some inkling what I'm talking about. But then again, there's only probably a handful of people reading this (#fuckyousocialmedianoonereadsanymore). At the time I had no idea wtf was going on or what I was doing – no reference points other than maybe something to do with da green stuff that I was smoking in those teenage kicks years. (Just as an aside I never did the mirror thing whilst stoned.)

Ok lets park that there.

Fast forward to 1990 and my Madchester years were in full swing. We'd dropped the THC for MDMA (ok so that was me trying to find a clever way to say us hipsters had stopped smoking pot and moved on [one] to Ecstasy). E blew our minds and then some. It opened our hearts and love was everywhere. I was living the dream working in the cooler-than-cool clothing shops in God's Own Land during the week, then shuffling my feet around the Hacienda nightclub dance floor at weekends with the help of ecstasy.

It's hard to say why anyone takes drugs but more often than not there's some kind of b(l)ack story. I have my own which I won't go into any kind of detail here , other than that I had a strange childhood that wasn't short of incident. Taking drugs is escapism. I was escaping and the high was a great place to escape to – what can be better than being in love with EVERYTHING.

But as the saying goes, every day has a night. And the start of my many, many nights was just around the corner.

I had moved up to Glasgow – this was about mid 1990. My best mate was living there and had told me about the crazy nightlife up north of the border. In 1990 Glasgow was awarded the European City of Culture. I had no idea what the criteria was to win this prestigious award but reckoned it had something to do with the quality of the ecstasy there. Part of being the European City of Culture meant that nightclubs were open until 5am – which was unheard of. In Manchester (and everywhere else in the country) the clubs closed at 2am and unless you went on the wild goose chase of trying to find a rave in a field, we had to go home and boogie. So the promise of good quality E combined with clubs until 5am was all it took. Adios Manchester. There is of course a b(l)ack story here. I was escaping from something that I only share with my therapists and priests.

What followed was a good few months of living for the E weekend as me mate Dave and me got off our 'eds every Saturday night – sometimes on a Friday too and even a rare Sunday. We were, as the saying goes, madfrit. When the music's over, turn off the light. Unfortunately for me, the music was never over as I relived the dream every weekend. Me mate Dave (who will always be referred to as me mate Dave!) had stopped going out. He wasn't quite as madfrit as I was. He had told me on a number of occasions that I should calm down and give it a miss on some weekends. And I didn't. The dream quickly cascaded into a nightmare. It was another Saturday night. They always followed the same path. Play a few tunes at home then wander into town. We lived literally 500 yards away from top Glasgow discotechque Sub Club. We would then wait for my man (the drug dealer) nervously for a few hours. Every weekend without fail there would be some cock and bull story why the drugs didn't turn up on time. This was the land before mobile phones. Eventually later than the allotted time – it was always later than the allotted time – our man turned up and we were ready for take off. Houston we have a problem. Half way through this one particular night it was fairly obvious that the good quality E we were regularly served up wasn't quite as good quality as normal. And unfortunately there wasn't any E trading standards we could complain too. I considered writing my MP but still had a bit of me wits about me. So instead I'd talk to our man himself:

Me to Drug Dealer 'E r mate this E is a bit shit tonight'

Drug Dealer to me 'Feck off ya wee dickhead'

Me to Drug Dealer 'Yes sir!"

The drug ecstasy is made up of a compound called MDMA. Pure MDMA is literally rocket fuel and guarantees a very good night. Unfortunately our aforementioned man wasn't too interested in giving you the best night out but only in making as much money as possible. Thus the pure MDMA was cut with all sorts of weird and wonderful things like paracetamol, uppers downers – whatever, as long as it was cheap and white.

I'd gone home early with a bee in my bonnet about my high being more biz than buzz (remember when we used that word biz as in, it's a bit biz that, meaning: a bit shit). I was playing Blue Lines, the classic Massive Attack album, when all of a sudden I began to experience a buzz. But this buzz was my heart going like the clappers. It wasn't very pleasant. I started to lose my shit a bit, not realising that I was in the midst of a drug induced panic attack. Me mate Dave handed me a couple of sleeping tablets to knock me out and the next thing I knew it was Sunday morning. Waking up I had tried to recollect the night before but it was all a little hazy. All I knew was I wasn't feeling my normal self. Well, it's quite normal not to feel normal after a night on the party meds. But this not normal definitely wasn't the normal not feeling normal – confused? So was I.

What followed over the coming weeks and months is the stuff of nightmares. Whenever I sit down to write I'm never 100 % sure what to write, just a vague idea. What I always try to do though is to add a little dash of humour – a little sugar to make the medicine go down. The next paragraph or two ain't got none of that.

Depersonalisation (DP) as a syndrome is an evolutionary tactic that the brain employs in moments of terror or panic. Say, for example, you were about to get knocked down by a car. Your brain would switch to depersonalise mode so it felt like it was someone else that was getting hit. Apparently, it's quite common for students going into an important exam to feel depersonalised, as though they were not in their own bodies, and it was someone else taking the exam. The DP symptoms are quite fleeting lasting only maybe 5-10 seconds, Depersonalisation Disorder (DPD) is when the person gets land locked in the symptoms and can't get out. Sometimes ever.

The morning after as described above was only a little unusual at first. Then it went to being somewhat strange. Finally leading into what would possibly be the worst several months of my life. And the first of 4 or 5 episodes in my life-long DPD struggles.

To give you some insight into DPD I often quote this piece on the net. I've found it to be the most insightful overview of the symptoms and how to explain them.

Depersonalization an insidious mental condition that can begin on its own ,it is the third most common psychiatric symptom, and it can also be a chronic disorder affecting more people than schizophrenia and bi-polar disorders combined. When it hits for the first time, you're convinced that you're going insane, and wait in a cold sweat to see when and if you finally do go over the edge.

The individual's perceptions of the self and the self's place in the world somehow shifts into a mindset that is altered from the norm, becoming hellish for most.

Depersonalization Disorder is a chronic illness that can take a dreadful and long-lasting course.

'A chronic illness that can take a dreadful and long-lasting course'

'Becoming hellish for most'

There's always a chance that writing something like this can turn into a 'pity party.' I don't want that. As mentioned in the opening I am writing as my mate suggested it could be cathartic – which to be honest is not really fucking happening. It really is difficult to find the right words to describe just how horrible DPD is – dreadful and hellish don't even begin to cover it. When you say to someone, well it's like I'm not real and my thoughts turn in on themselves, and it feels strange actually being a person that talks eats etc, the usual response is 'oh that sounds a little weird." It's not a little weird, it really is hell on earth. Scratch that, whatever's beneath hell, it's that on earth. I cannot really in any way, shape, or form describe how bad it is. Have you ever had a panic attack? Or maybe even a bad LSD trip or similar – well you're getting nearer the symptoms here – except the panic attack goes on for weeks, months, years in some cases.

During that first DPD in Glasgow in 1993 I went from doctor to doctor trying to find answers, getting fed different medications – none of which I would take. I was too paranoid the meds would make things worse. I gave up tea, coffee, and alcohol. Needless to say I stopped the E too. It got so bad that I was afraid to eat sweets, scared that the additives in them would make the symptoms even worse. The French philosopher Jean-Paul Satre described it as 'The Filth' – which for a bite-size descriptive is not half bad.

The move back to Manchester came quickly as I looked for comfort and support from my family. They arranged for me to see a local doctor who had no idea what I was talking about – neither did any of the psychologists. After seeing maybe 3 or 4 different doctors I was finally admitted into the psychiatric department at Stepping Hill Hospital in Stockport for 'observation.' It was here that a certain Dr. Dumar diagnosed me with DPD. And the cure? 'Well Mr. Ryan there isn't a specific cure. We've got medication for the anxiety and depression that DPD causes but at the moment there is nothing else that can help directly with it.' A combination of street drugs with a healthy dose of childhood trauma seemed to be the cocktail that kicked things off.

Over the next 6-12 months and being settled back in Manchester, the DPD symptoms eased up and I was able to continue with some kind of normality. The DP symptoms were there but were lurking in the background. I tried various things including reflexology, which helped a little but it was mainly a time thing that made the symptoms ease up. I got super fit. I ran a lot. Exercise was good for the mind as well as the body. And it was exercise, albeit with an Asian twist, which would play a big part in my rehabilitation in my next DPD episode in my late twenties when a friend suggested Yoga.

I am now 53. My last experience of DPD was in my late thirties. I thought I was done with it for good. Boy was I wrong. In the last 10 years I have got married, had 2 more children, moved from Manchester to Los Angeles, Los Angeles to London, London to Manchester, Manchester back to Los Angeles, Los Angeles to Deal (Kent), and finally Deal to Ramsgate. 6 months ago with the toll of all this moving around, and lots of other things, I separated from my wife. I managed the stress for a while – perhaps I stuffed some of it in a sack. But unfortunately everything caught up with me and the DPD returned. And when the going gets tough as the saying goes, the tough redoubles their efforts. More Yoga, some running, cold water swimming, eating healthy – all these things help but there's no magic bullet. As my late father used to say, All you can do son is white knuckle ride it out. I've spent half my adult life on a DPD white knuckle ride and I want to say I've kicked it's ass. But that's not the truth. To be honest, at the moment it feels as if it's kicked mine over and over again. And then again for good measure.

I wanted to end the blog on the above paragraph, but I think there must be some kind of resolution to it, and a nod to the blogs title: "The drugs don't work but the Ashtanga does." All things must pass, sang George Harrison. Eckhart Tolle said, 'Sometimes there doesn't seem like a way out, but there's always a way through.' I know at some point the DP symptoms will pass. I've no idea when that some point will be. But in the meantime, I'll be using (as I've used many times before) Ashtanga Yoga to help me find the way through.

Say a little prayer for me.

Shit happens

October 2016

A good few years back I was listening to a podcast by a Buddhist teacher. A student had asked him how he would react in a rather tense hypothetical situation, the student was obviously expecting the teacher to say he'd be all 'zen' and not get stressed out. But this teacher didn't say that , he went into detail about it's hard to know how anyone would react until they were actually in any kind of situation and all the meditation practice in the world might not prove to be of any help at all in certain circumstances. Yesterday I had one of those circumstances.

After a rather lovely 2 weeks in Sweden with my wife and 2 kids I decided to nip back to Blighty to see some family ,some mates and also make sure my Yoga Empire* was behaving itself. Being the rather thoughtful soul I am, I took Easy my 2 year old nutcase with me – with Lina (wife) and Boo (5 going on 15 year old daughter) heading back to LA. After a weeks' worth of Manchester and 2 days in London, Easy and I headed to Gatwick for the 14.10 eleven hour and twenty minute schlep on Norwegian Airlines back to LA. I had food, water, lollipops, IPad , paper and crayons – basically the works for any normal 2 year old on a long haul flight- what possibly could go wrong.

After being in the air literally 5 minutes Easy** had managed to knock a cup of water all over my groin area which made me looked like I'd wet myself. I was chair bound until it dried off – cheers son. But this was very small beer compared to what the little sod had in store for me not too long after. He nodded off for a while which gave me the opportunity to listen to some zen podcast about zen – my favourite pastime. I realise this might sound a bit boring to some people but It's pretty crazy stuff I kid you not(ok it is boring). After a rather shorter snooze than I'd hoped for Easy was awake and ready to twist my melon big time. We were playing 'lets draw all over dad's favourite music magazine game when I smelled something rather unpleasant. My heart dropped, 'maybe he's just farted' I thought clutching at a bag of big straws. I pushed him forwards to see my worst fears being realised 5000 feet in the air. The dreaded BP (BP is short for bath poo , my wife and I came up with this – it's basically when your kid does a number two and the only way to deal with it is to stick them in the bath – fully clothed). But this was not just a normal BP this was BPXL and then some. I quickly picked him up underneath his armpits held him as far away from myself as I could trying to ensure I didn't actually knock him into another passenger , and marched into the smallest space possible for a toilet. If there was a soundtrack to this story think Ave Santini (Omen theme tune).I stood him on the toilet lid and stripped him down to the buff – it was literally everywhere and I mean EVERYWHERE – it had murdered the nappy he was wearing and was down his legs into his socks and up his back. I had to play the the child poo version of Operation (google if you don't know this game it'll make sense) trying to ensure as I unclothed him that the 3 layers of number twos that covered his tops and bottoms didn't cover any further body parts – big fat fail. It got wiped on his ears his chin in his hair and of course Easy wanted to add his own soundtrack to all this by wailing as loud as possible so anyone passing would think I was shoving hot pins in his backside.

Things got worse.
Obviously I had to try and clean his caked clothes with only a wash basin fit for Tom Thumb to do it in. Oh and how is the drainage system in the aforementioned wash basin – why it's a load of shit Matt I hear you say. Yes so now I had a screaming child and a wash basin full of water with brown floaties (I'm sorry for the kiddie manure minutiae here but the small details are important). It wasn't draining and I couldn't have walked out of the cubicle leaving it to fester. I saw a bottle of hand wash and had the genius idea of pouring out the soap and using the empty bottle to scoop up the soiled water and pour it down the toilet. Ok I got Easy off the toilet and stood him in the far corner of the modest bathroom (this is Estate Agent speak for 'the bathroom is fecking tiny mate ') and proceeded to unscrew the top of the hand wash. Except it wouldn't unscrew. I yanked and yanked until BOOM the top came off and out came the hand soap literally covering every bit of me and Easy (and cubicle ceiling) that wasn't already covered in crap. Oh happy days. If there was a human car wash on the plane I would have been sorted but there wasn't #obvs. I'd like to say at this point to all those of you reading this who don't have kids but are thinking about it , please don't let this blog put you off – it's really ace. So after literally the best part of an hour of cleaning and scooping and washing (and Easy's wailing) we were ready to go back to our seats. So at this point I realised I didn't actually have any more clothes for him except for another nappy (a nappy is a diaper for all my US brothers and sisters) and another pair of pants. I put all his washed but still stinking clothes into some sick bags and gave him my tee-shirt to wear. At least I had a jacket which I had to put on and zip up – didn't think it would serve any purpose going for that unzipped Miami Vice jacket over bare skin vibe. We sat down exhausted and still smelling despite my best efforts with 2 bags of wet wipes and the hand soap scraped off the toilet walls.

It got worse.

Ten minutes later he did the same thing again, I kid you not. It wasn't quite the Armageddon shit show I'd just experienced but it wasn't far off. Back to the toilet washing him down etc – you get the jist by now. Except this time there was a massive big fat problem – no more clothes – the tee that I had given him to wear was washed and sentenced to the sick shit bag and I was facing the real dilemma of arriving into the US and having to go through immigration with Easy wearing nothing but my summer jacket and me naked from the waist up. You can just picture the very lovely officers at the US Immigration being totally understanding... NOT – we'd have been put on the next plane back to London. Help came to our rescue when I decided to speak to the cabin crew – I'm having an emergency situation I said to a young chap – he took one look at my shell-shocked face and felt my pain. He sat us down and went and got a tee and pair of shorts from his own luggage for Easy – it was too big but given the potential shirtless immigration situation I was facing I'd make it work. I managed to blag a couple of nappies from a couple with a small baby and forced Easy into them. I think he wanted to complain given the size of the tiny nappy but even he at 2 years old could see in my eyes that one more peep from him and I was jumping out the plane.

We landed not long after and got through immigration without too much fuss – even though Easy looked like some kind of hippy child in his body length Kaftan tee-shirt. So coming back to the first paragraph of hypothetical situations – I'm sure you'd expect someone like me who has done plenty of yoga and meditation to be able to be totally zen in the above 'shit happens ' predicament but the truth is that I lost my shit big time (after being covered in it) Hey I'm not perfect sue me 😜 Please try not think of any of this when I'm adjusting you next.

*of course this is a complete joke -anyone who is on the inside of Yoga Manchester , Yoga Express and Yoga London Club will tell you we are the Namaste Fawlty Towers and I am Guru Fawlty.

** ok any idiot who decided to call their kid Easy get what they deserve.. I now know this.

#The blog title Shit Happens was inspired by Buddhist teacher Stephen Batchelor who reframed the Buddha's first noble truth of life is suffering / there is suffering to the more contemporary 'Shit Happens'!

Printed in Great Britain
by Amazon

23309436R00040